ACTION ORIGAMI

Paper Toys that Fly, Hop, Twirl, Shake and Surprise!

Isamu Sasagawa

TUTTLE Publishing

Tokyo | Rutland, Vermont | Singapore

Table of Contents

Basic Folds and Symbols   6

 Chapter 1: Funny Faces and Silly Poses

Munching Mouth	10	
Fake Mustache	12	
Blinking Eyes	14	
Wagging Tongue	16	
Tooth and Toothbrush	18	
Funny Uncle	20	
Laughing Santa Claus	22	
Push-up Pro	24	
Sit-up Champ	26	
Cheeky Moves	28	
I Beg Your Pardon!	30	
Crawling Baby	32	
Cheerleader Shaking Pom-Poms	34	
Thumbs Up!	36	
The Maestro	38	

Welcome to the world of Action Origami!

This book contains origami that you can move, play with, use to make your friends laugh and surprise people. You can also follow along with the accompanying videos on YouTube, so you can fold as much as you want. These models are funny, fun and unique—they're the best!

—Isamu Sasagawa

Chapter 2 — Amazing Magic Tricks

Snake-in-the-Box	40
Scary Shell	42
Magic Candy	44
Magic Ice Cream	46
Momotaro's Peach	48
Transforming Princess Fuji	50
Magic Rising Chair	52

Use round stickers effectively!

This book features many creations with eyes and mouths. If you use the round stickers sold at craft or office supply stores as well as dollar stores, you can make eyes and mouths easily! You can cut them in half, layer stickers of different colors and sizes, and be creative to make fun faces. Of course, you can also draw them on if you prefer!

Chapter 3 — Otherworldly Origami

Lantern Ghost Sticking Out Its Tongue	54
Chattering Skull	56
Gyrating Ghost	58
Staggering Zombie	60
Flapping Bat	62
Kappa Eating a Fish	64
Rattling Lizard Cryptid	66
Jumping Sea Monster	68
Ninja Throwing a Star	70
Slicing Samurai	72
Munching Monster	74
Transforming Alien	76

Chapter 4: Awesome Toys

Spinning Poop		78
Self-Destruct Button (1)		79
Self-Destruct Button (2)		80
Flexible Sword		82
Power Shovel Arm		84
Kickable Cleats		86
Catapult		88
Spinning Shuriken		90
Spinning Shooting Star		92
Tree-Go-Round		93
Roly-Poly Toy		94
Jumping Airplane		95
Spinning Propeller		96
Mount Fuji Airplane		98
Whale Airplane		100
Tumbling UFO		101
Flying Squirrel Airplane		102

How to View the Video Lessons

To access the how-to videos
1. Make sure you have an Internet connection.
2. Enter the URL below into your web browser.

tuttlepublishing.com/action-origami

For support, you can email us at info@tuttlepublishing.com.
Kids: If you don't understand, please ask an adult for help.

Please Note
- There are sometimes minor differences between the details in the book and what is shown in the videos.
- The videos may be removed without notice.

Chapter 5: Cute Chibi Animals

Monkey Playing Cymbals	104	
Jumping Caterpillar	106	
Charging Wild Boar & Rhino	108	
Headstand Penguin	110	
Elephant with Raisable Trunk	112	
Bouncing Squid	114	
Dancing Octopus	116	
Swimming Dolphin	118	
Happy Squirrel	120	
Howling Dog	122	
Flipping Frog	124	
Owl Opening Its Eyes	125	
Lovey-Dovey Fox	126	
Eating Monkey	128	
Gliding Cat	130	
Pecking Woodpecker	132	
Gliding Ray	134	
Somersault Seal	136	
Munching Fish	138	
Swimming Sunfish	140	

Origami Bases

Blintz Base	141
Boat Base	141
8-Row Precrease (1)	142
8-Row Precrease (2)	142
Fish Base	143
Balloon Base	143
Crane Base	144

Index 145

Basic Folds and Symbols

The folding diagrams that are used to describe how objects are folded have various symbols on them. If you memorize them, folding origami becomes easy.

Valley Fold

Fold the paper so that the dashed line become a "valley."

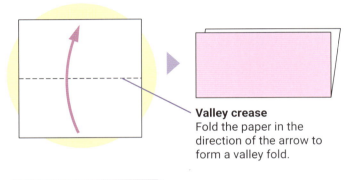

Valley crease
Fold the paper in the direction of the arrow to form a valley fold.

Mountain Fold

Fold the paper at the dashed line so that the paper becomes a "mountain" toward the outside.

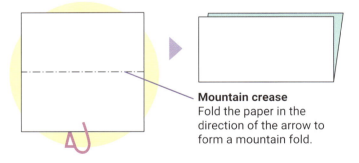

Mountain crease
Fold the paper in the direction of the arrow to form a mountain fold.

Press Firmly with Your Fingers Like an Iron!

Press and slide your fingers firmly along creases as if you were ironing them. This way, the creases will be sharp and straight.

Make a Crease

If you fold the paper once and then open it up again, a crease is made that becomes a guideline for the next fold.

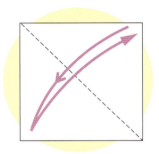

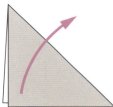

1 After making a valley fold in the direction of the arrow, unfold the paper to return it to its original state.

2 A crease has formed where you folded.

Open Up and Flatten

■ Open Up a Square and Flatten

Place a finger into the square pocket indicated by the squat up arrow ⬆. Then, open up the paper in the direction of the long arrow and flatten.

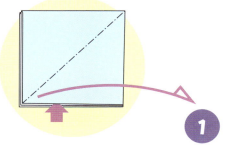

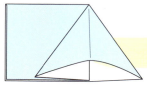

1 A finger has been inserted into the square pocket and the pocket has been opened up.

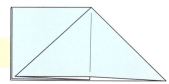

2 Flatten the pocket and it transforms into a triangle!

▲ Open Up a Triangle and Flatten

Place your fingers in the triangular pocket indicated by the squat up arrows ⬆. Then, open up the paper in the direction of the long arrow and flatten.

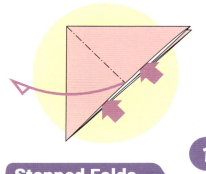

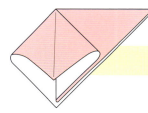

1 Fingers have been inserted into the triangular pocket and the pocket has been opened up.

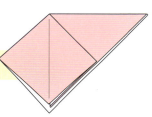

2 Flatten the pocket and it transforms into a square!

Stepped Folds

Make a mountain fold and a valley fold next to each other so that the folds form a "step" or "pleat."

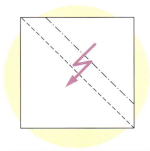

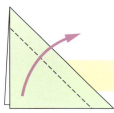

1 After having folded the paper in half with a valley fold first, fold the paper back at the dashed line.

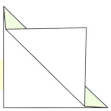

2 The mountain fold and the valley fold are next to each other, forming a "step."

Make Horns

Make points like horns at the corners indicated with double arrows ⩓.

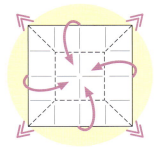

▶

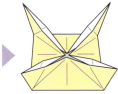

If you fold the paper in the direction of the arrows, "horns" (triangular flaps) will be formed.

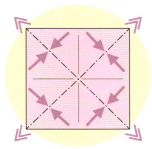

▶

Pinch the double-arrow ⩓ corners to form "horns."

7

Inside Reverse Fold

Pop a folded corner inside out.

Press with your fingers to fold it in.

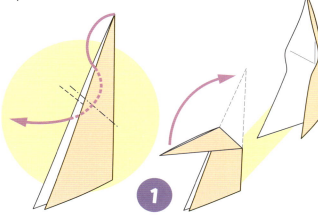

1. Make a fold at the dashed line and open it up again to make a crease.
2. Open up the paper a little, and then fold the paper inward at the crease.
3. Fold down more....
4. The inside reverse fold is completed.

Outside Reverse Fold

Invert a corner to the outside along a crease.

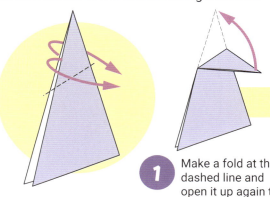

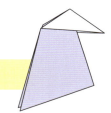

1. Make a fold at the dashed line and open it up again to make a crease.
2. Open up the first fold, and turn the paper over to the outside at the crease made in step ①.
3. Once it's folded down, the outside reverse fold is completed.

Reorganize Layers

Expose a side of the paper that is different from the side you were folding.

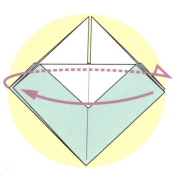
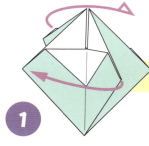
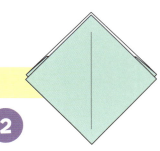

1. Fold the front side to the left, and the back side to the right.
2. Different sides from the ones you were folding have been exposed.

Chapter 1
Funny Faces and Silly Poses

Munching Mouth

Clamp it in your mouth and chomp down! You'll find yourself making a funny face.

If you hold it against your open mouth while inhaling through it gently, it will stay in place!

VIDEO Enter this URL into your browser: **tuttlepublishing.com/action-origami**

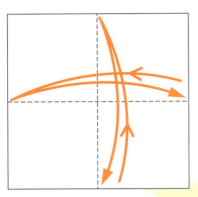

1 Fold the paper in half edge to edge both ways and unfold to make 2 creases.

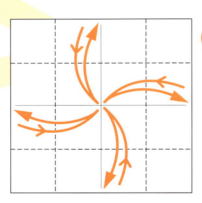

2 Fold each edge to the center and unfold to make creases.

Step ② is completed. Turn the paper over.

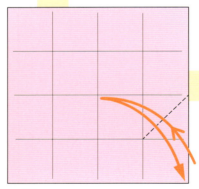

3 Align the bottom-right corner with the center, and make a crease only where indicated by the dashed line.

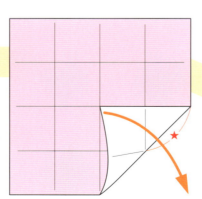

Step ③ in progress. Once you have installed a crease in the span indicated by the ★ symbol, unfold the flap.

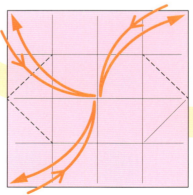

4 In the same way, make creases at the 3 dashed locations. Turn the paper over.

10 Chapter 1

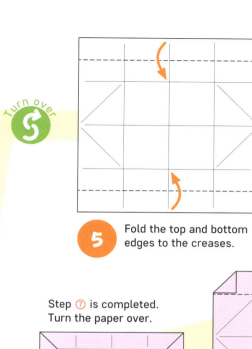

5 Fold the top and bottom edges to the creases.

Step ⑤ is completed. Turn the paper over.

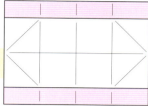

6 Fold the 4 corners inward to align with the creases.

Step ⑦ is completed. Turn the paper over.

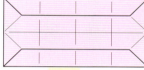

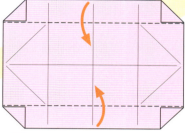

7 Fold along the existing creases at the top and bottom.

Flip it over and put it in your mouth!

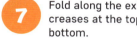

8 Use the existing creases to fold both sides into triangles, and fold them toward the center.

Step ⑧ in progress.

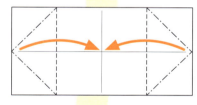

Finished

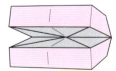

Gaaah!

It's a scary mouth!

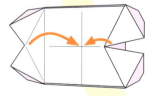

9 Fold the paper in half at the center.

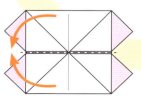

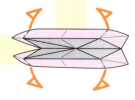

10 Fold at the 4 points to create right-angle corners and make it three-dimensional.

If it's too big, make it with origami paper that's trimmed to a smaller size.

Funny Faces and Silly Poses   11

Fake Mustache

[Ahem, ahem!] Look at me, I'm a big deal!

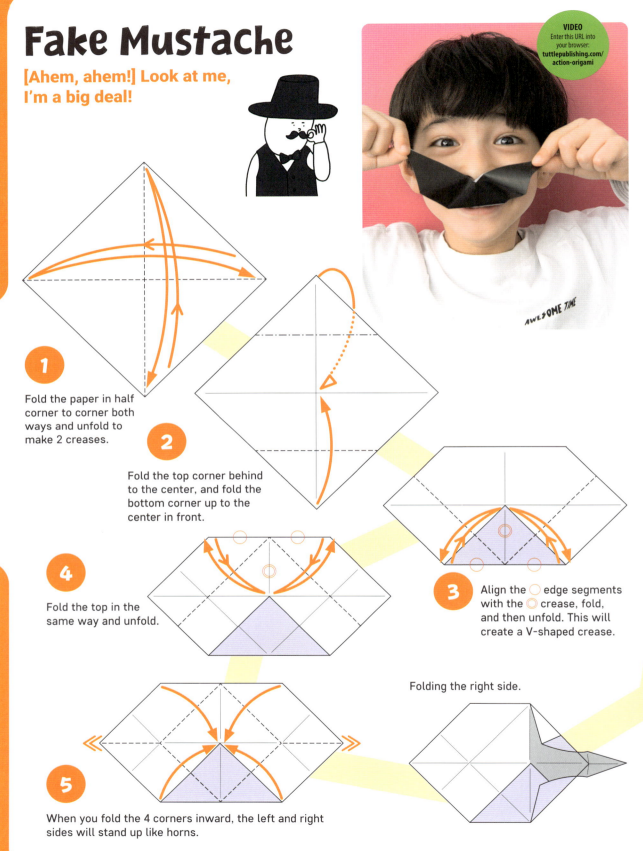

1 Fold the paper in half corner to corner both ways and unfold to make 2 creases.

2 Fold the top corner behind to the center, and fold the bottom corner up to the center in front.

3 Align the ○ edge segments with the ○ crease, fold, and then unfold. This will create a V-shaped crease.

Folding the right side.

4 Fold the top in the same way and unfold.

5 When you fold the 4 corners inward, the left and right sides will stand up like horns.

12　Chapter 1

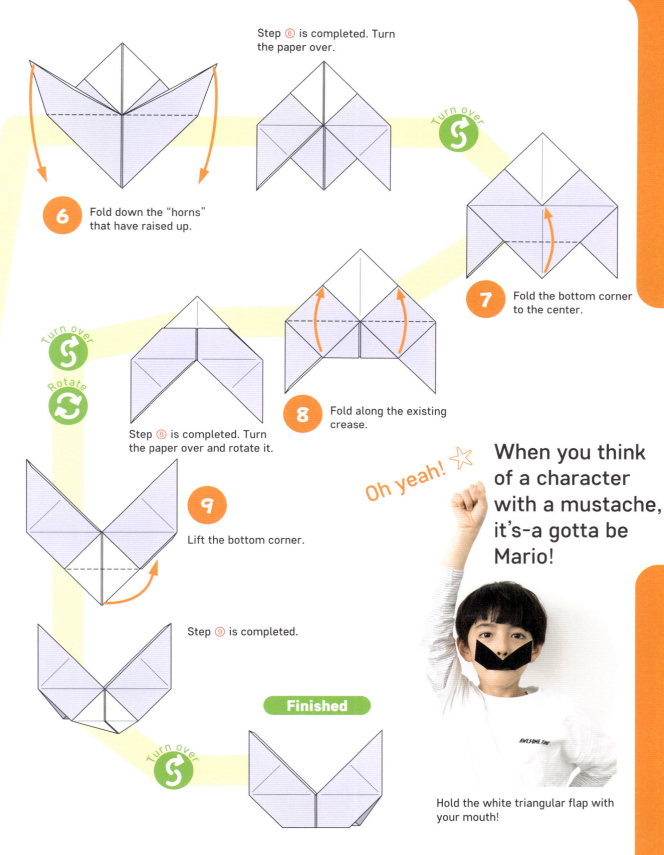

6 Fold down the "horns" that have raised up.

Step ⑥ is completed. Turn the paper over.

7 Fold the bottom corner to the center.

8 Fold along the existing crease.

Step ⑧ is completed. Turn the paper over and rotate it.

9 Lift the bottom corner.

Step ⑨ is completed.

Finished

Oh yeah! When you think of a character with a mustache, it's-a gotta be Mario!

Hold the white triangular flap with your mouth!

Funny Faces and Silly Poses 13

Blinking Eyes

Flex this model to make faces with silly squints or wide-eyed wonder.

Hold both ends, and move your hands together and apart.

VIDEO
Enter this URL into your browser:
tuttlepublishing.com/action-origami

Fold up to step ② of an 8-Row Precrease (2) (see page 142).

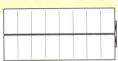

Small gap.

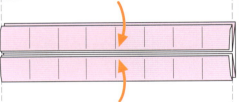

1 **Fold** in the top and bottom edges, leaving a gap in the middle.

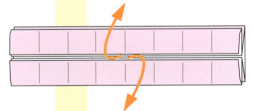

2 **Open** the overlapping parts together to reveal the inner surface.

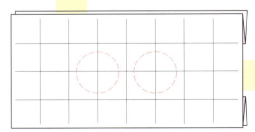

3 Color in 2 eye spots in the areas indicated by the dashed lines.

Turn over

5 Fold diagonally both ways and unfold in the shaded squares as shown to form an X-shaped crease.

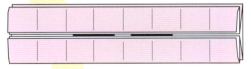

Step ④ is completed. Turn the paper over.

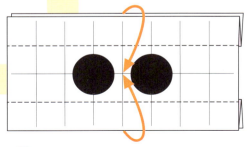

4 Return the parts that were opened.

14 Chapter 1

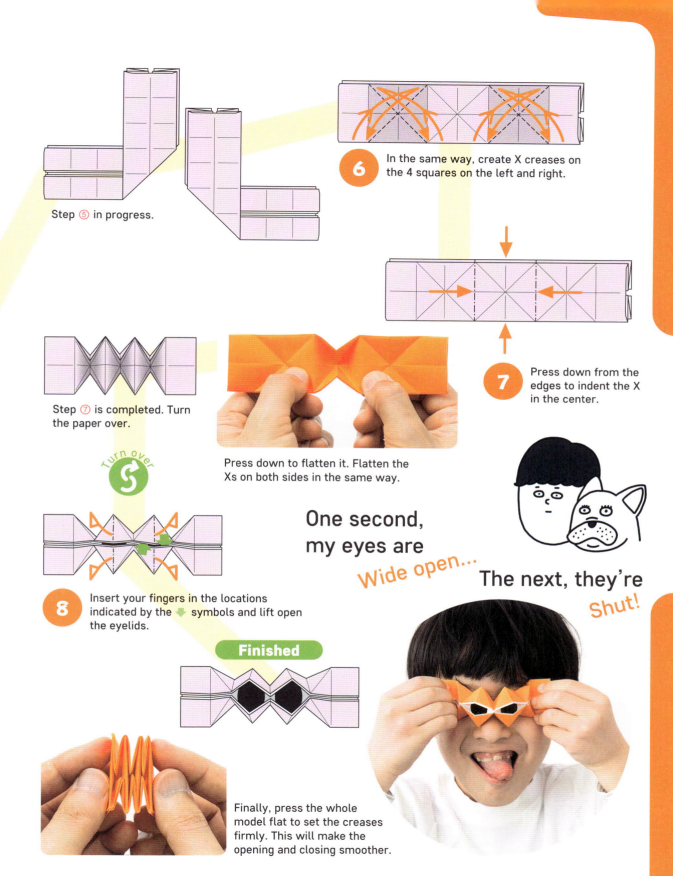

Step ⑤ in progress.

6 In the same way, create X creases on the 4 squares on the left and right.

7 Press down from the edges to indent the X in the center.

Step ⑦ is completed. Turn the paper over.

Press down to flatten it. Flatten the Xs on both sides in the same way.

One second, my eyes are *Wide open...* The next, they're *Shut!*

8 Insert your fingers in the locations indicated by the ⬇ symbols and lift open the eyelids.

Finished

Finally, press the whole model flat to set the creases firmly. This will make the opening and closing smoother.

Funny Faces and Silly Poses   15

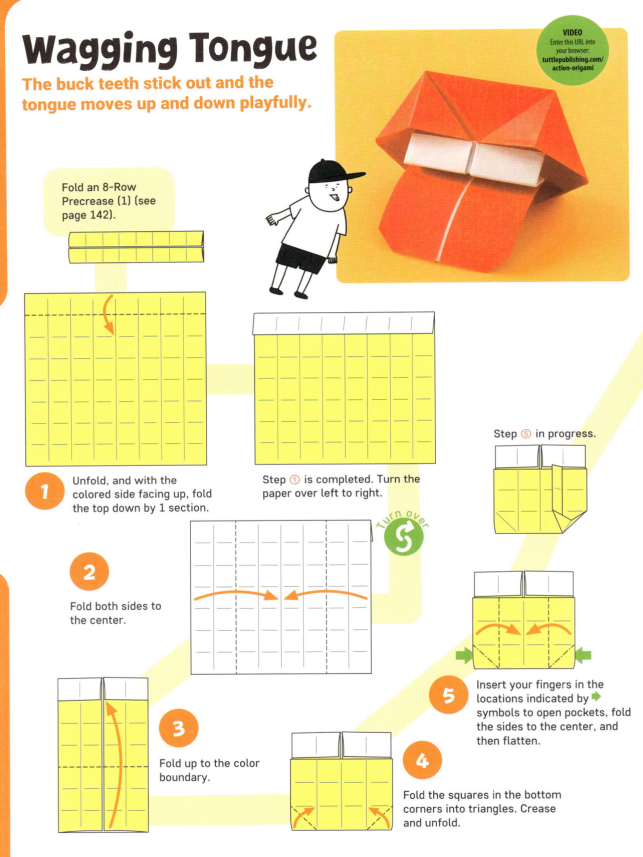

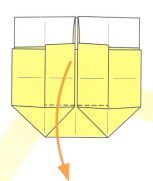

6 Fold down the part you just folded.

7 Fold the entire top portion down along the dashed line.

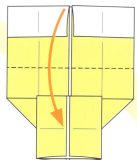

Stick out the tongue!!

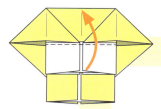

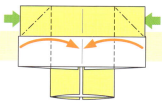

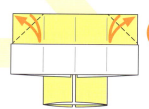

8 Fold the squares in the top corners into triangles. Crease and unfold.

10 Fold up the white part. This will become the front teeth.

9 Insert your fingers in the locations indicated by ➡ symbols to open pockets, fold the sides to the center, and then flatten.

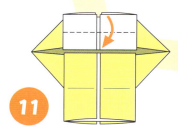

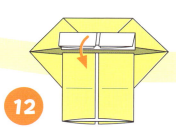

11 Fold the front teeth in half.

12 Swing the front teeth downward.

13 Fold small portions of the bottom corners to the back.

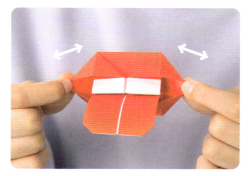

Hold both ends and move them to make the tongue wiggle and extend.

Adding a curve to the tongue will make it look more realistic!

Finished

Funny Faces and Silly Poses   17

Tooth and Toothbrush

Even if you brush these teeth diligently, it's no substitute for brushing your actual teeth!

Tooth

Fold an 8-Row Precrease (1) (see page 142).

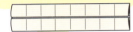

1 Open it all the way, and then fold it in half.

2 Make creases at 4 locations.

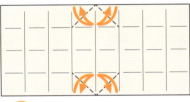

3 Firmly fold and unfold each side adjacent to the central vertical crease.

Lift the bottom right corner up. Make a diagonal crease only along the span indicated by the ★ symbol. Unfold. Do the same for the other 3 locations.

4 Firmly fold and unfold each side adjacent to the central horizontal crease.

5 Fold both sides inward by 1 square.

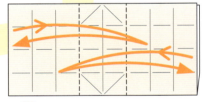

6 Fold all 4 corner squares in half diagonally.

Scrub away that tartar!

Chapter 1

Toothbrush

Fold an 8-Row Precrease (2) (see page 142).

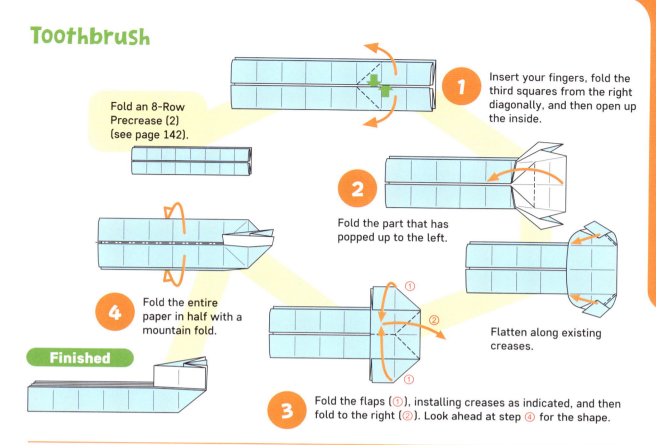

1 Insert your fingers, fold the third squares from the right diagonally, and then open up the inside.

2 Fold the part that has popped up to the left.

Flatten along existing creases.

3 Fold the flaps (①), installing creases as indicated, and then fold to the right (②). Look ahead at step ④ for the shape.

4 Fold the entire paper in half with a mountain fold.

Finished

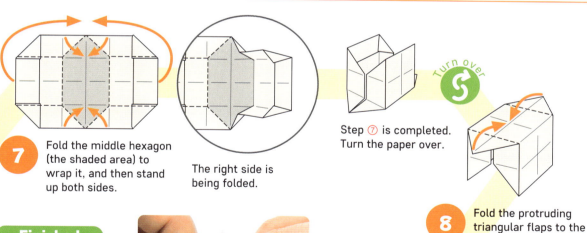

7 Fold the middle hexagon (the shaded area) to wrap it, and then stand up both sides.

The right side is being folded.

Step ⑦ is completed. Turn the paper over.

8 Fold the protruding triangular flaps to the middle to shape it into a box.

9 While pressing down in the center, flatten the entire shape into an X.

Finished

Insert your fingers from beneath and mostly restore the shape, leaving some of the indentation.

Flattening from the outside, press firmly to compress the form.

Funny Faces and Silly Poses

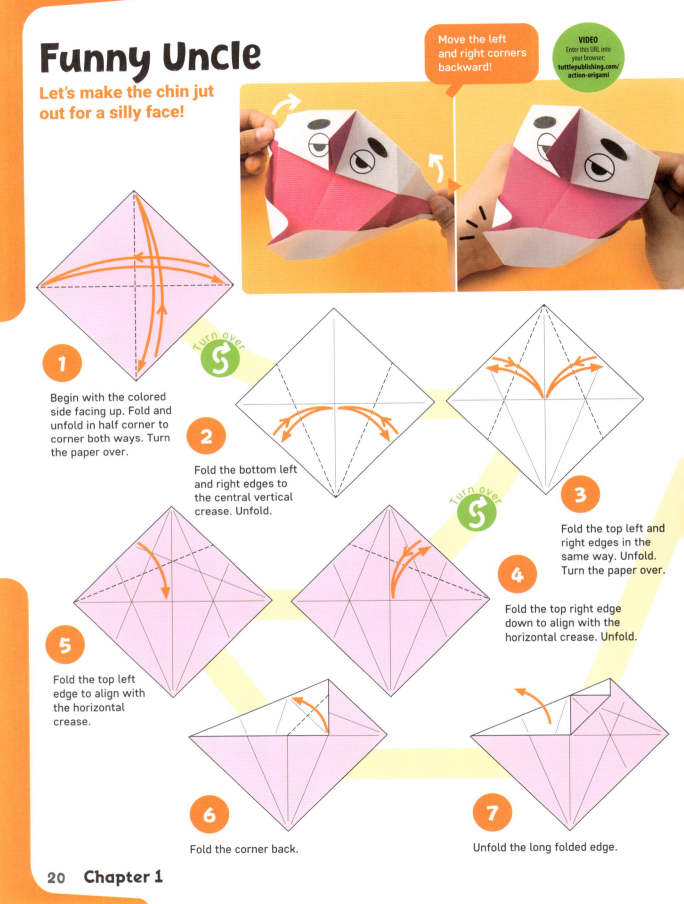

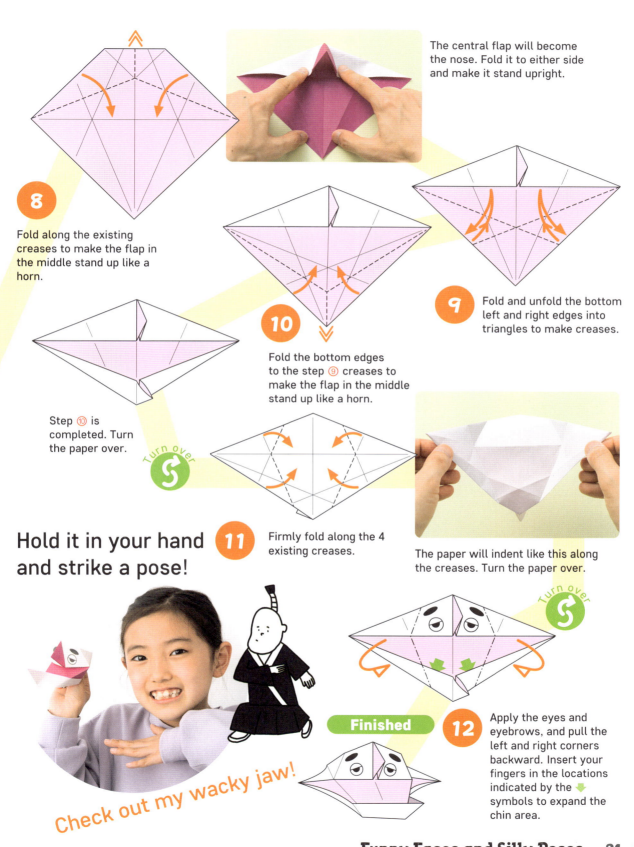

8 Fold along the existing creases to make the flap in the middle stand up like a horn.

The central flap will become the nose. Fold it to either side and make it stand upright.

9 Fold and unfold the bottom left and right edges into triangles to make creases.

10 Fold the bottom edges to the step ⑨ creases to make the flap in the middle stand up like a horn.

Step ⑩ is completed. Turn the paper over.

11 Firmly fold along the 4 existing creases.

The paper will indent like this along the creases. Turn the paper over.

Hold it in your hand and strike a pose!

Check out my wacky jaw!

Finished

12 Apply the eyes and eyebrows, and pull the left and right corners backward. Insert your fingers in the locations indicated by the ⬇ symbols to expand the chin area.

Funny Faces and Silly Poses 21

Laughing Santa Claus

He shakes his beard and laughs. You can almost hear him saying, "Ho ho ho!"

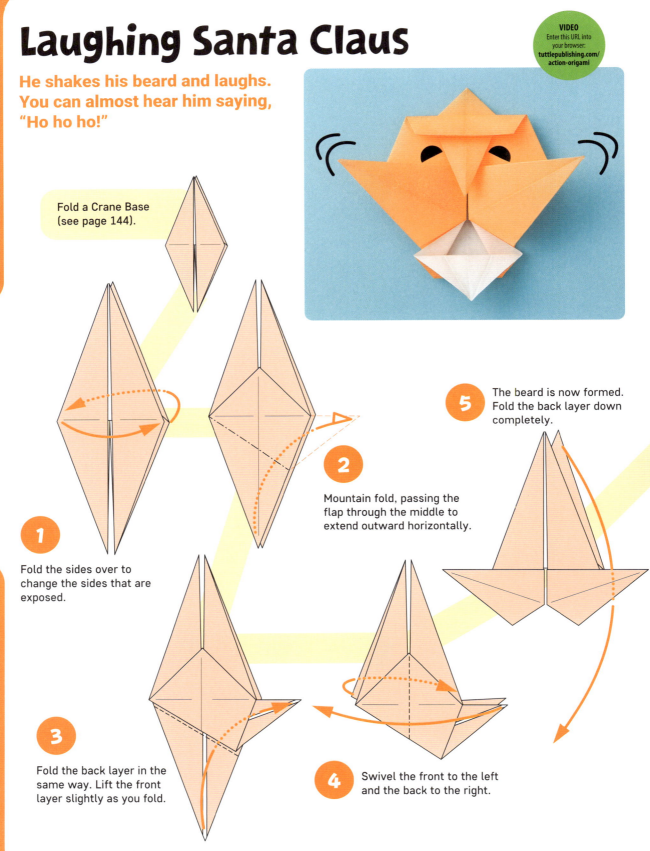

Fold a Crane Base (see page 144).

1 Fold the sides over to change the sides that are exposed.

2 Mountain fold, passing the flap through the middle to extend outward horizontally.

3 Fold the back layer in the same way. Lift the front layer slightly as you fold.

4 Swivel the front to the left and the back to the right.

5 The beard is now formed. Fold the back layer down completely.

VIDEO
Enter this URL into your browser:
tuttlepublishing.com/action-origami

22   Chapter 1

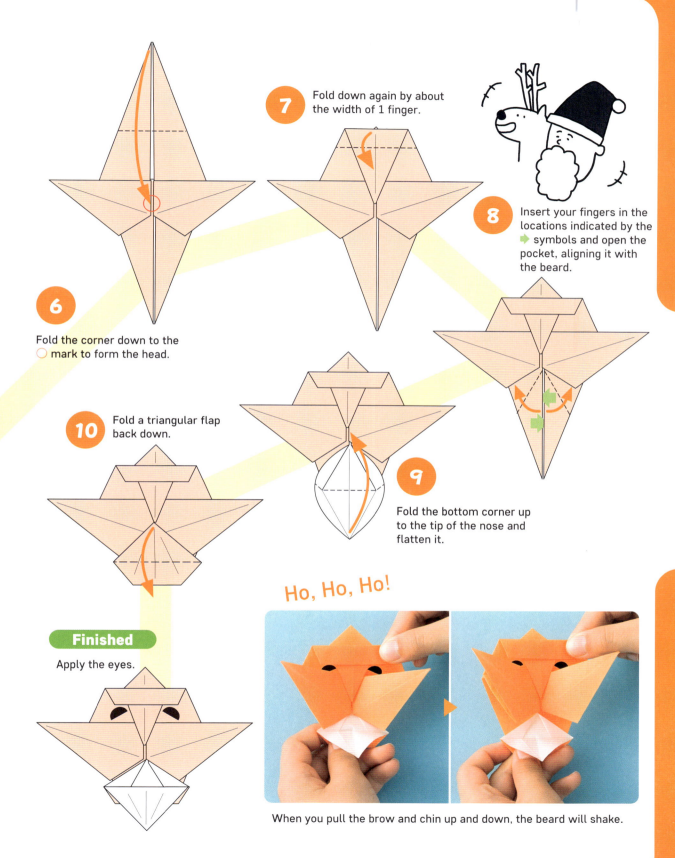

Funny Faces and Silly Poses 23

Push-up Pro

Press the back, 1-2-3-4! Even exhausting push-ups are easy with this model!

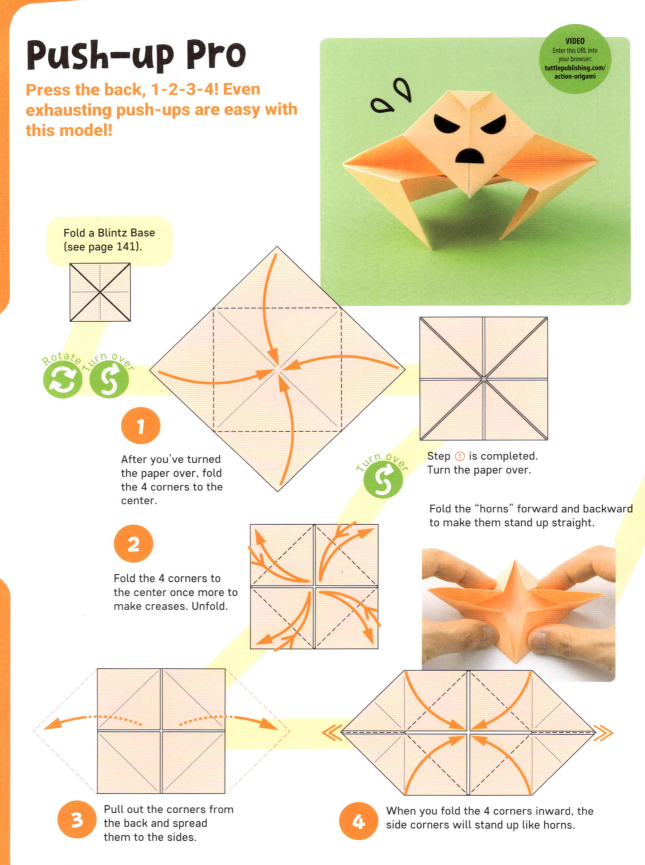

Fold a Blintz Base (see page 141).

Rotate / Turn over

1 After you've turned the paper over, fold the 4 corners to the center.

Turn over

Step ① is completed. Turn the paper over.

2 Fold the 4 corners to the center once more to make creases. Unfold.

Fold the "horns" forward and backward to make them stand up straight.

3 Pull out the corners from the back and spread them to the sides.

4 When you fold the 4 corners inward, the side corners will stand up like horns.

24 Chapter 1

Step ④ is completed.

Flattening the right side.

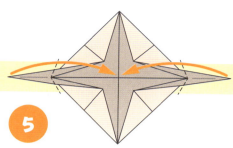

5 Insert your fingers into the side flaps, open them up, and flatten them into squares.

Both sides have been flattened. Turn the paper over.

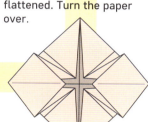

Turn over

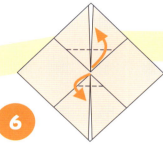

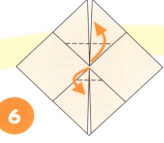

7 Apply eyes and a mouth to the lower square to create a face.

6 Fold 2 corners: fold the top corner larger to form the shorts, and the bottom corner smaller to form the hair.

8 Open the pockets underneath to form arms.

Yo!

Ho!

Ha!

Place your finger on the waistband area of the shorts and press the body down.

Finished

Shorts

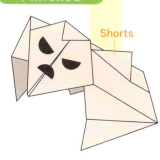

You can do as many reps as you want with this enthusiastic fitness buff!

Funny Faces and Silly Poses 25

Sit-up Champ

One, two! One, two! Train your abs and get ripped!

Fold a Crane Base (see page 144).

1 Rotate 180°. Fold the front left flap to the right, and the back right flap to the left to expose new layers.

2 Cut only the front flap to the middle.

3 Make mountain folds and pass the flaps through the inside, so the tips point the sides.

4 The arms are done. Fold diagonally upward to form the elbows.

Push the knees with your fingers!

26　Chapter 1

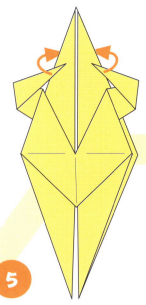

5

Tuck the folded tips behind. It will look as if the hands are clasped behind the neck.

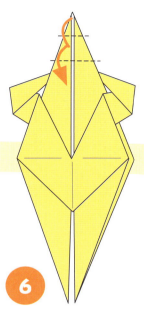

6

Fold the top corner twice to form the face.

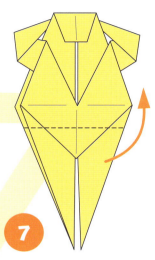

7

Fold the body in half along the dashed line.

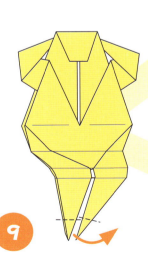

9

Fold small portions of the tips to form the ankles and feet.

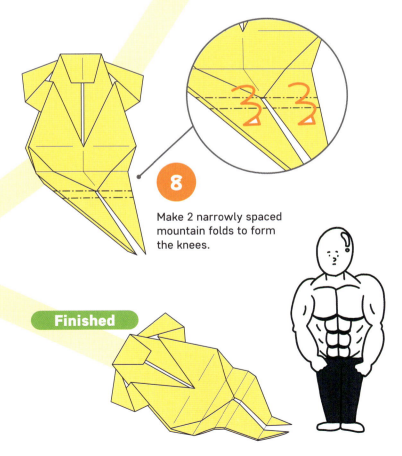

8

Make 2 narrowly spaced mountain folds to form the knees.

Finished

Funny Faces and Silly Poses 27

Cheeky Moves

Get ready for some laughs, because this model is about to cause an irreverent rump-us!

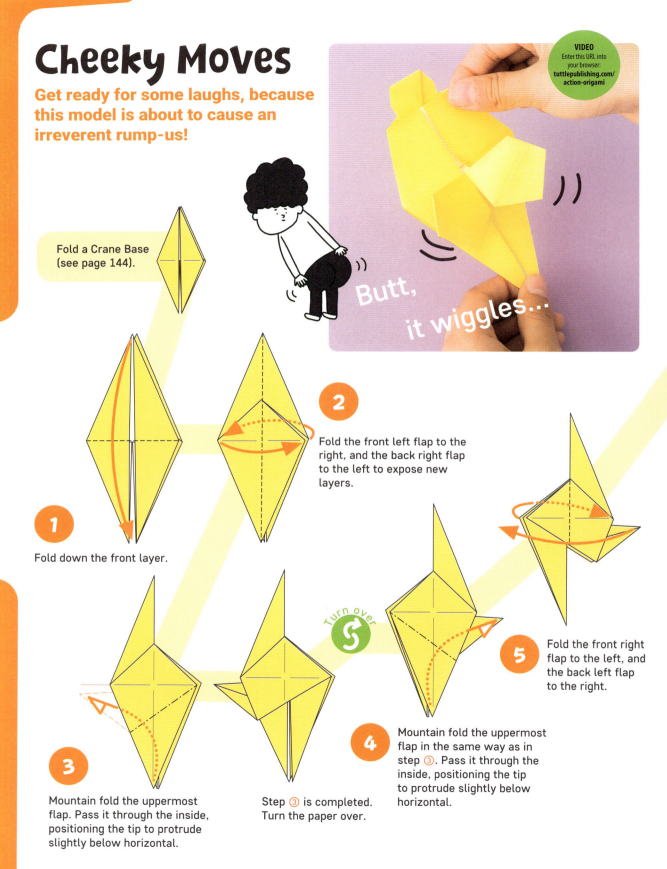

Butt, it wiggles...

VIDEO Enter this URL into your browser: tuttlepublishing.com/action-origami

Fold a Crane Base (see page 144).

1 Fold down the front layer.

2 Fold the front left flap to the right, and the back right flap to the left to expose new layers.

3 Mountain fold the uppermost flap. Pass it through the inside, positioning the tip to protrude slightly below horizontal.

Step ③ is completed. Turn the paper over.

4 Mountain fold the uppermost flap in the same way as in step ③. Pass it through the inside, positioning the tip to protrude slightly below horizontal.

5 Fold the front right flap to the left, and the back left flap to the right.

28 Chapter 1

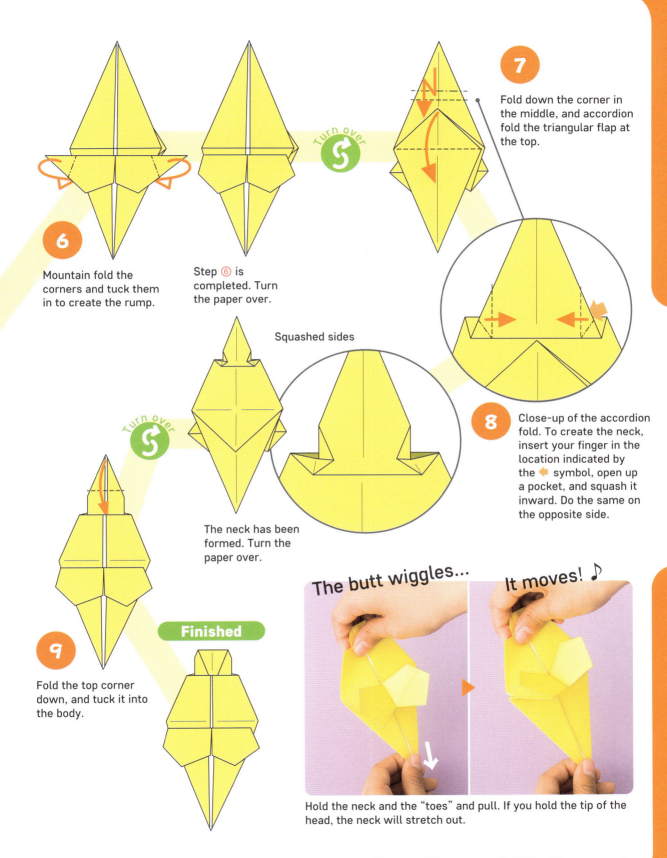

Funny Faces and Silly Poses 29

I Beg Your Pardon!

You can try having this origami apologize or kowtow on your behalf... but if the gesture ends up causing problems, don't blame me!

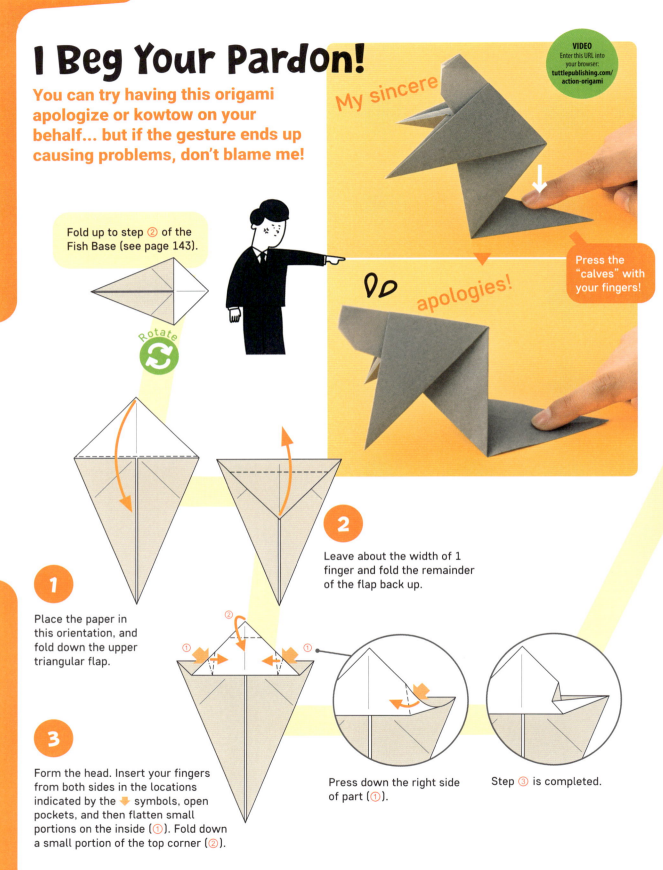

VIDEO Enter this URL into your browser: tuttlepublishing.com/action-origami

My sincere apologies!

Press the "calves" with your fingers!

Fold up to step ② of the Fish Base (see page 143).

Rotate

1 Place the paper in this orientation, and fold down the upper triangular flap.

2 Leave about the width of 1 finger and fold the remainder of the flap back up.

3 Form the head. Insert your fingers from both sides in the locations indicated by the ⬇ symbols, open pockets, and then flatten small portions on the inside (①). Fold down a small portion of the top corner (②).

Press down the right side of part (①).

Step ③ is completed.

30 **Chapter 1**

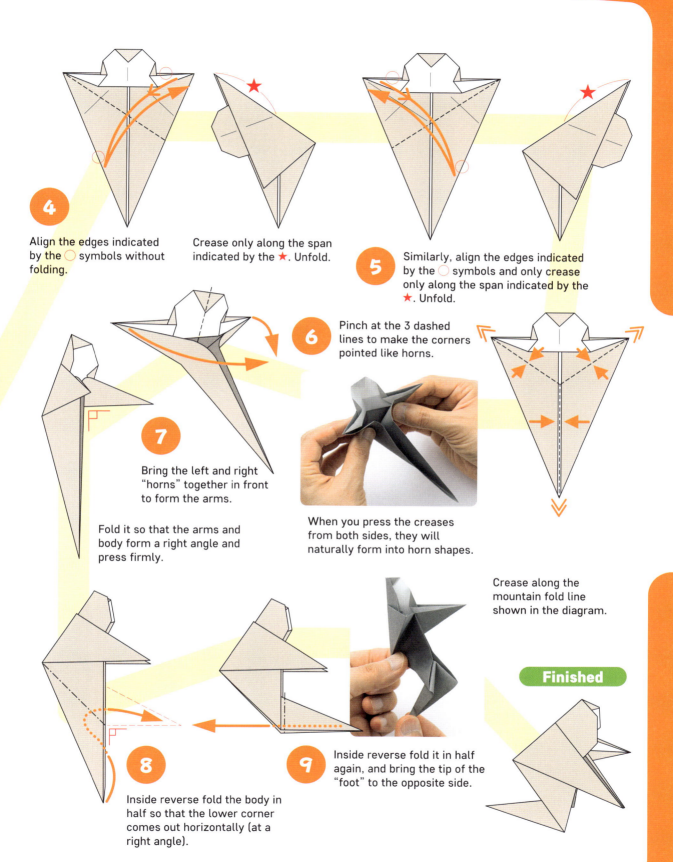

Funny Faces and Silly Poses

Crawling Baby

It crawls while shaking its big head and bottom.

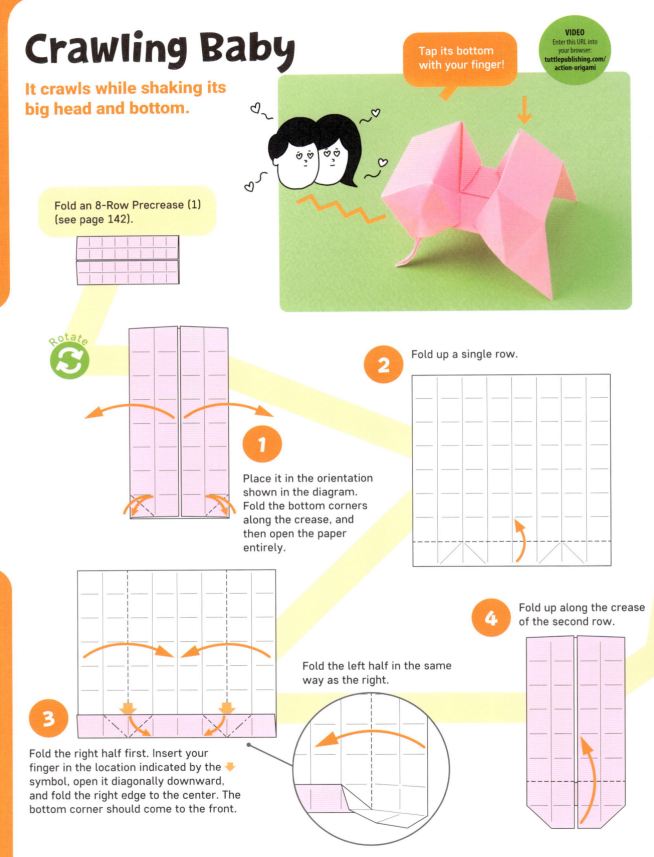

Tap its bottom with your finger!

VIDEO Enter this URL into your browser: tuttlepublishing.com/action-origami

Fold an 8-Row Precrease (1) (see page 142).

1 Place it in the orientation shown in the diagram. Fold the bottom corners along the crease, and then open the paper entirely.

2 Fold up a single row.

3 Fold the right half first. Insert your finger in the location indicated by the ⬇ symbol, open it diagonally downward, and fold the right edge to the center. The bottom corner should come to the front.

Fold the left half in the same way as the right.

4 Fold up along the crease of the second row.

32 Chapter 1

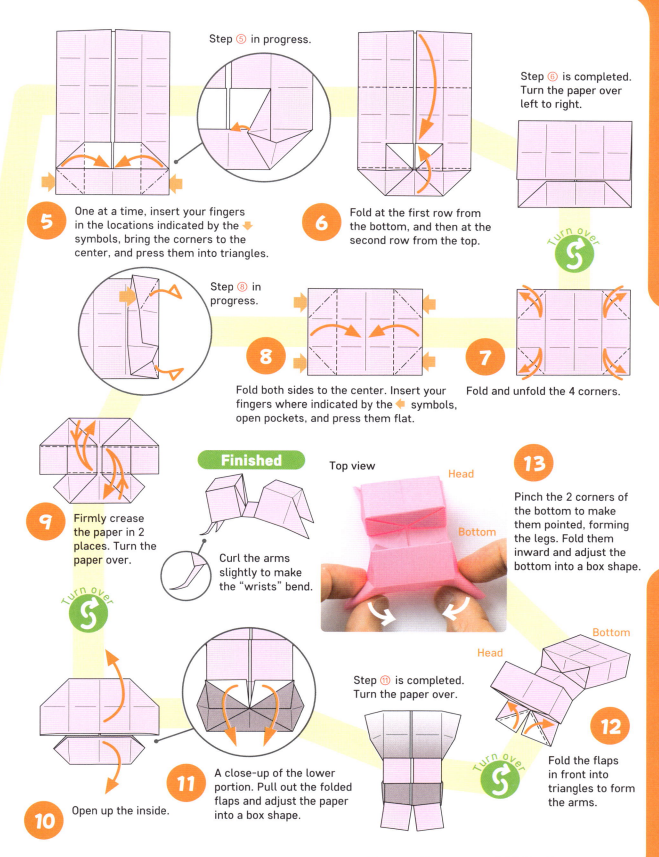

Funny Faces and Silly Poses 33

Cheerleader Shaking Pom-Poms

Shake these pompoms to show support for the team!

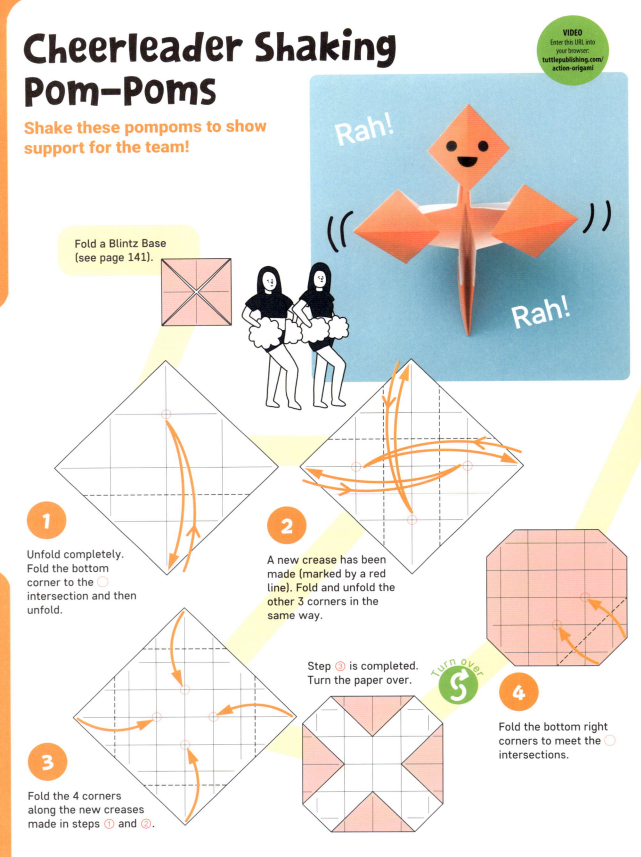

Fold a Blintz Base (see page 141).

1 Unfold completely. Fold the bottom corner to the ◯ intersection and then unfold.

2 A new crease has been made (marked by a red line). Fold and unfold the other 3 corners in the same way.

3 Fold the 4 corners along the new creases made in steps ① and ②.

Step ③ is completed. Turn the paper over.

4 Fold the bottom right corners to meet the ◯ intersections.

VIDEO
Enter this URL into your browser:
tuttlepublishing.com/action-origami

34 Chapter 1

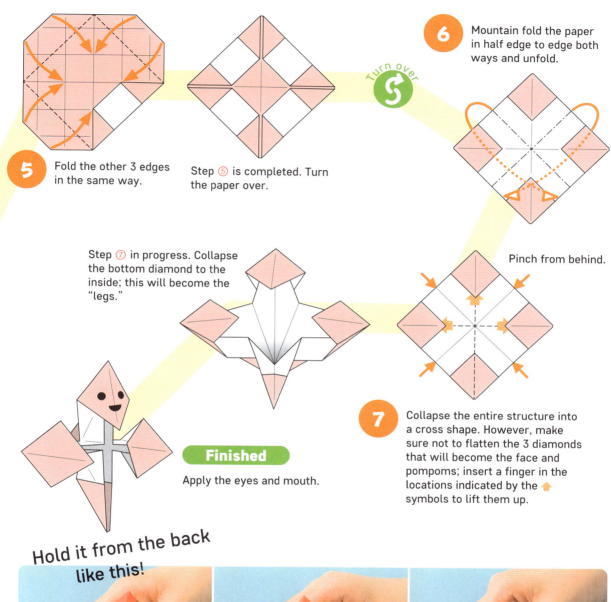

5 Fold the other 3 edges in the same way.

Step **5** is completed. Turn the paper over.

Turn over

6 Mountain fold the paper in half edge to edge both ways and unfold.

Pinch from behind.

Step **7** in progress. Collapse the bottom diamond to the inside; this will become the "legs."

7 Collapse the entire structure into a cross shape. However, make sure not to flatten the 3 diamonds that will become the face and pompoms; insert a finger in the locations indicated by the symbols to lift them up.

Finished

Apply the eyes and mouth.

Hold it from the back like this!

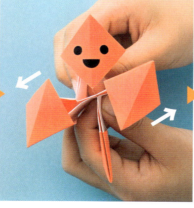

▲ Hold the upper and lower body separately.

▲ Rub the upper and lower parts together quickly side to side to make the pom-poms move.

Funny Faces and Silly Poses 35

Thumbs Up!

Let's give lots of "Likes!" With this handy model, your thumb won't get tired!

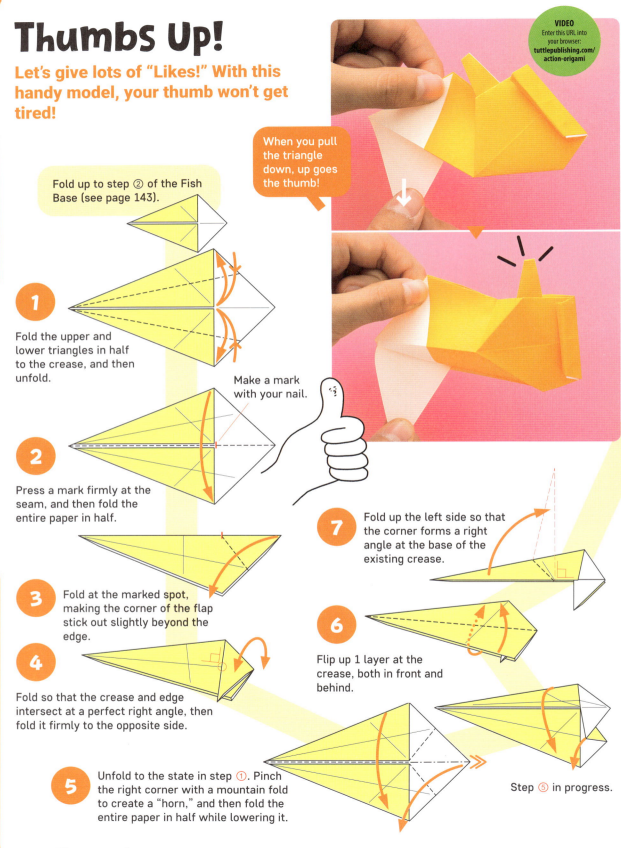

VIDEO
Enter this URL into your browser:
tuttlepublishing.com/action-origami

When you pull the triangle down, up goes the thumb!

Fold up to step ② of the Fish Base (see page 143).

1 Fold the upper and lower triangles in half to the crease, and then unfold.

2 Press a mark firmly at the seam, and then fold the entire paper in half.

Make a mark with your nail.

3 Fold at the marked spot, making the corner of the flap stick out slightly beyond the edge.

4 Fold so that the crease and edge intersect at a perfect right angle, then fold it firmly to the opposite side.

5 Unfold to the state in step ①. Pinch the right corner with a mountain fold to create a "horn," and then fold the entire paper in half while lowering it.

6 Flip up 1 layer at the crease, both in front and behind.

7 Fold up the left side so that the corner forms a right angle at the base of the existing crease.

Step ⑤ in progress.

36 **Chapter 1**

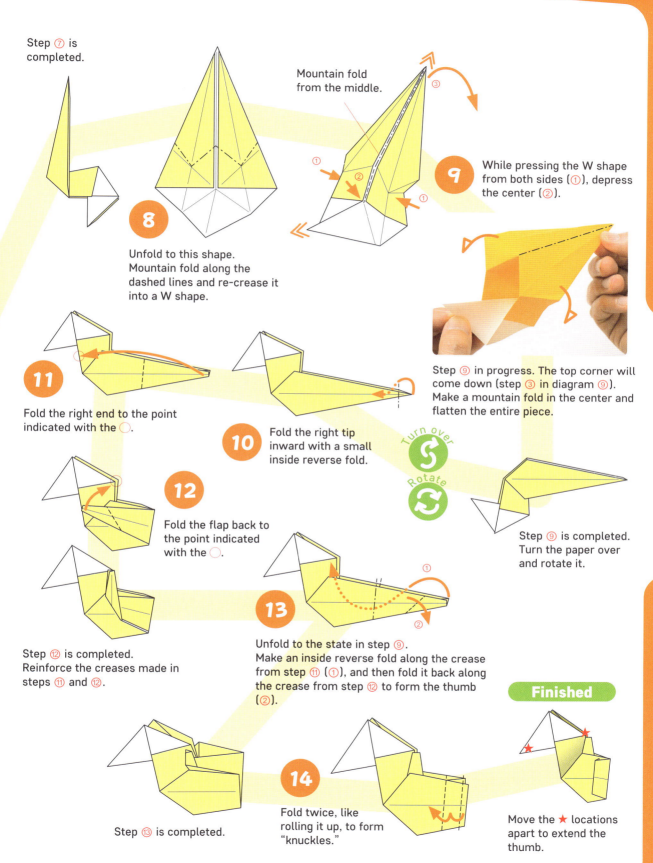

Funny Faces and Silly Poses 37

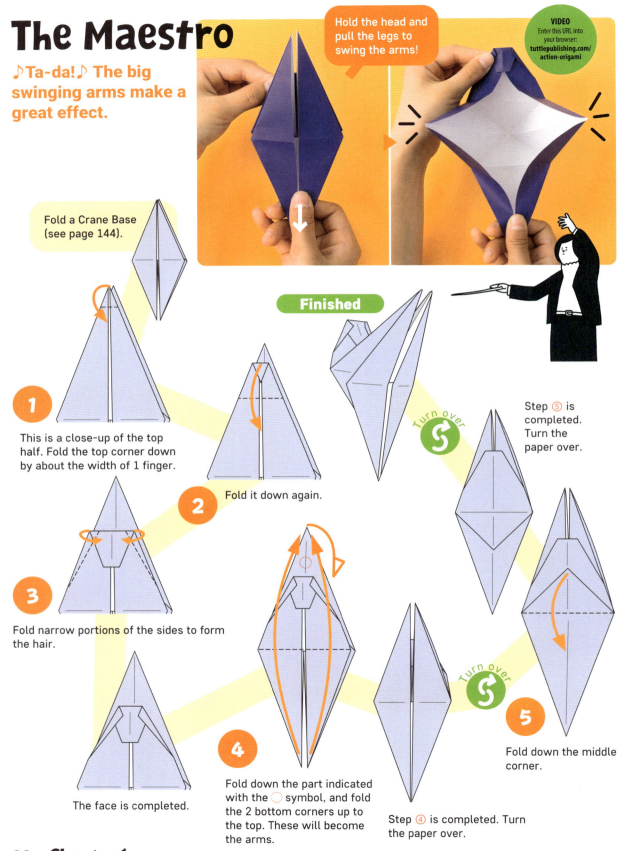

Chapter 2 Amazing Magic Tricks

Snake-in-the-Box

It's a jack-in-the-box with a snake that stretches out. Surprise your friends!

When you loosen your grip on the box...

[Boiiing!]

VIDEO Type this URL into your browser: tuttlepublishing.com/action-origami

Fold an 8-Row Precrease (1) (see page 142).

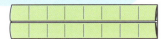

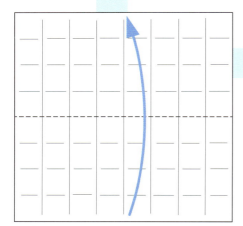

1 Unfold the entire paper, and then fold it in half.

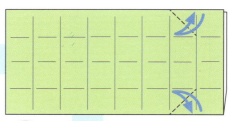

2 Create diagonal creases at the top and bottom of the second column.

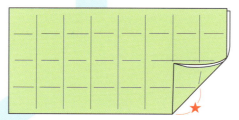

Step ② in progress. Fold the square into a triangle, creasing only along the span indicated by the ★ symbol, and then unfold. Do the same with the square at the top.

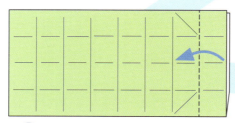

3 Fold in the first column on the right.

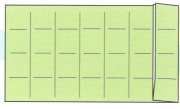

Step ③ is completed. Turn the paper over.

Turn over

40   Chapter 2

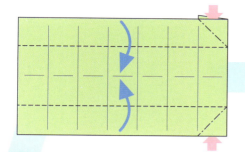

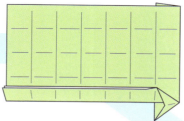

Step ④ in progress at the bottom. Do the same at the top.

5 Fold the 2 left corners into triangles. Unfold. Turn the paper over.

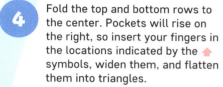

4 Fold the top and bottom rows to the center. Pockets will rise on the right, so insert your fingers in the locations indicated by the ⬆ symbols, widen them, and flatten them into triangles.

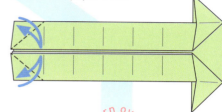

Step ⑥ in progress.

Turn over

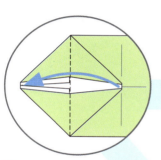

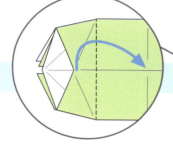

7 Fold the flap back to the left, forming a triangle.

6 Insert your finger in the location indicated by the ➡ symbol, and fold inward and flatten only the front layer.

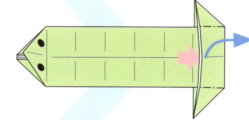

8 Apply eyes to the triangle on the left. Insert your finger in the location indicated by with the ➡ symbol. Lift open the pocket, and shape it into a box.

Finished

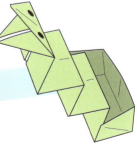

9 Fold the rectangular span in an accordion pattern with alternating mountain and valley folds, then collapse the paper into the box.

Lower the head and firmly press both sides with your fingers to keep the snake from popping out until you're ready to spring your surprise!

Amazing Magic Tricks

Scary Shell

If you put your finger into the clam with its shell wide open... Wow! It clamps down and won't let go!

Clamping clam shells?! Maybe just stay in bed!

Fold an 8-Row Precrease (1) (see page 142).

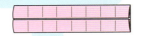

1 Open the upper layers to the outside, forming this shape. Fold the 4 corners in along the creases.

2 Fold in small portions of the sides of the corners from step ① to further round the shape.

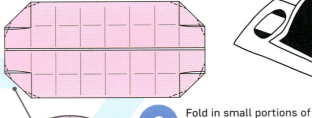

A close-up of the corner. Just fold in small portions.

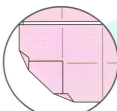

Step ② is completed.

4 The step ③ crease (the red line) has been installed. Do the same in the other 3 corresponding locations to install diagonal creases.

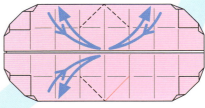

3 Add a diagonal crease next to the center crease.

Step ③ in progress. Fold the right side, creasing only along the span indicated by the ★ symbol, and then unfold.

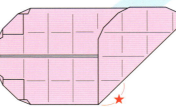

42 Chapter 2

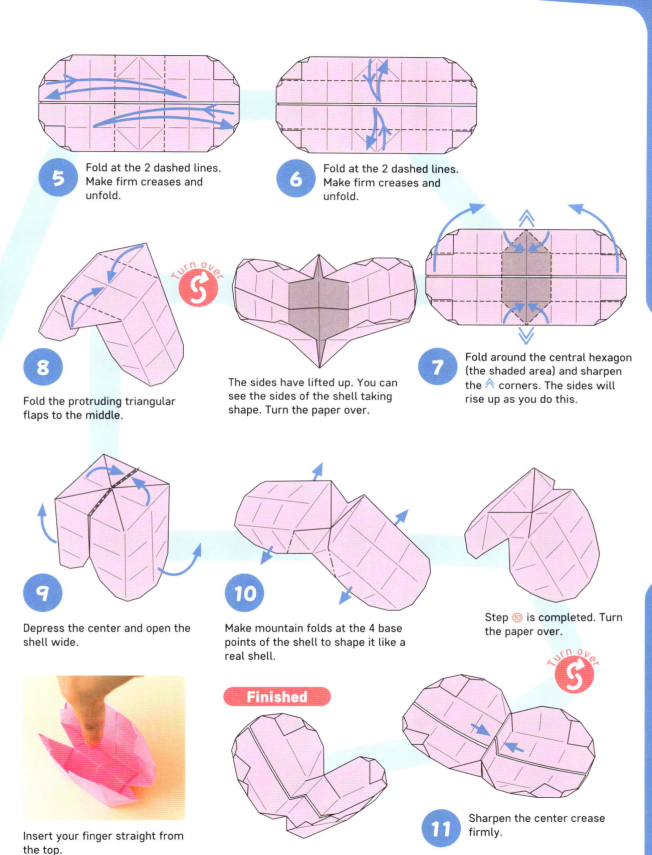

Amazing Magic Tricks 43

Magic Candy

It's a wonderful treat that never runs out, no matter how much you appear to eat!

Fold an 8-Row Precrease (2) (see page 142).

1

After you've turned the paper over, make V-shaped creases on the third squares from each side.

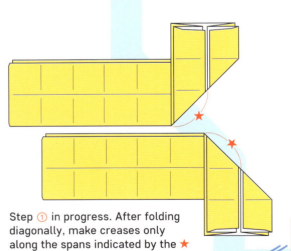

Step ① in progress. After folding diagonally, make creases only along the spans indicated by the ★ symbols, and then unfold. Fold the left side in the same way.

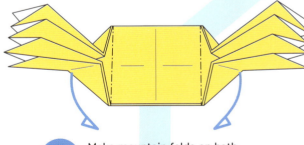

3 Make mountain folds on both sides of the center square.

2 Fold around the central hexagon (the shaded area). As the sides rise up, bundle the layers together.

44   Chapter 2

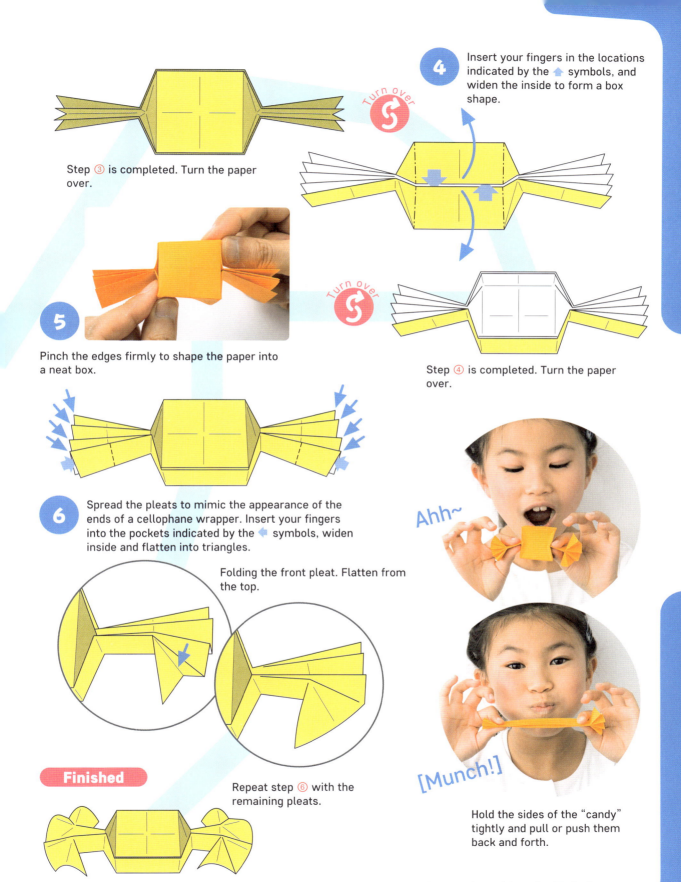

Amazing Magic Tricks 45

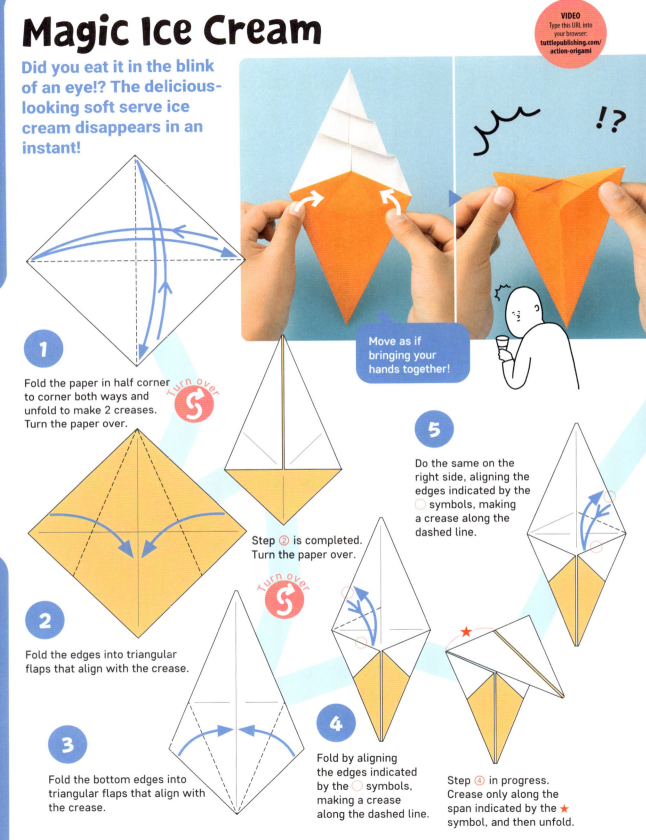

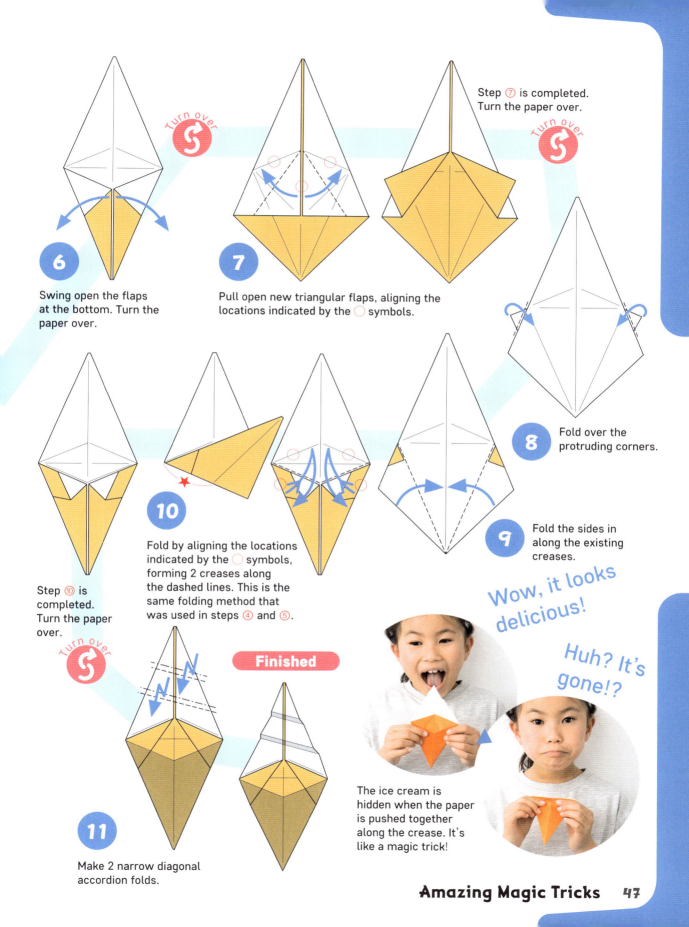

Amazing Magic Tricks 47

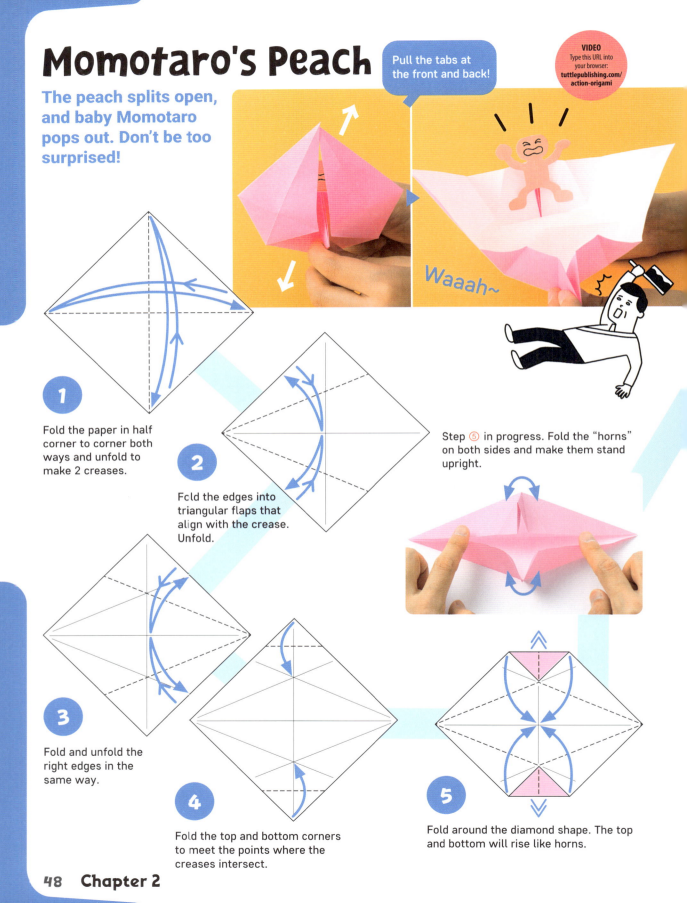

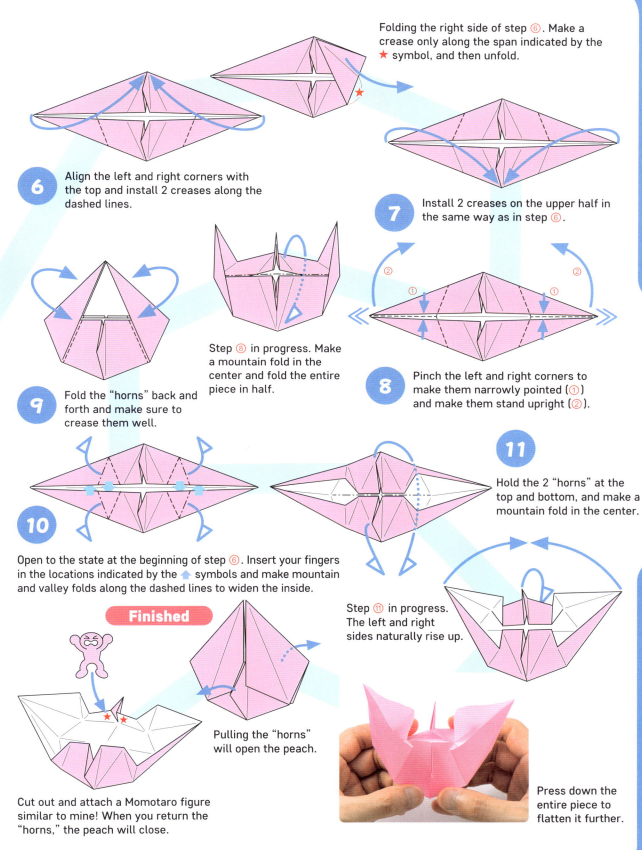

Amazing Magic Tricks 49

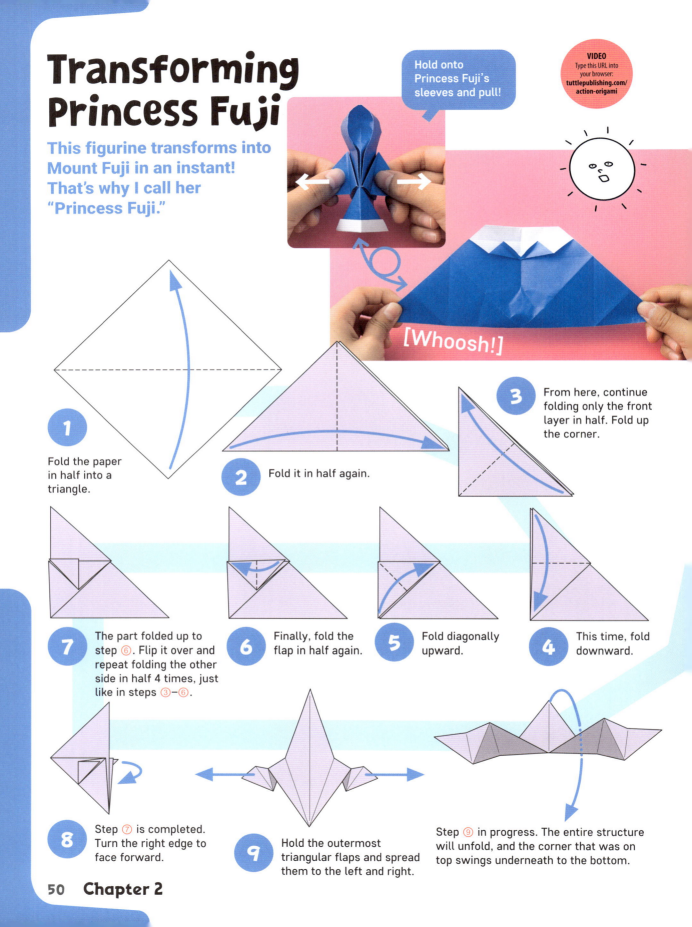

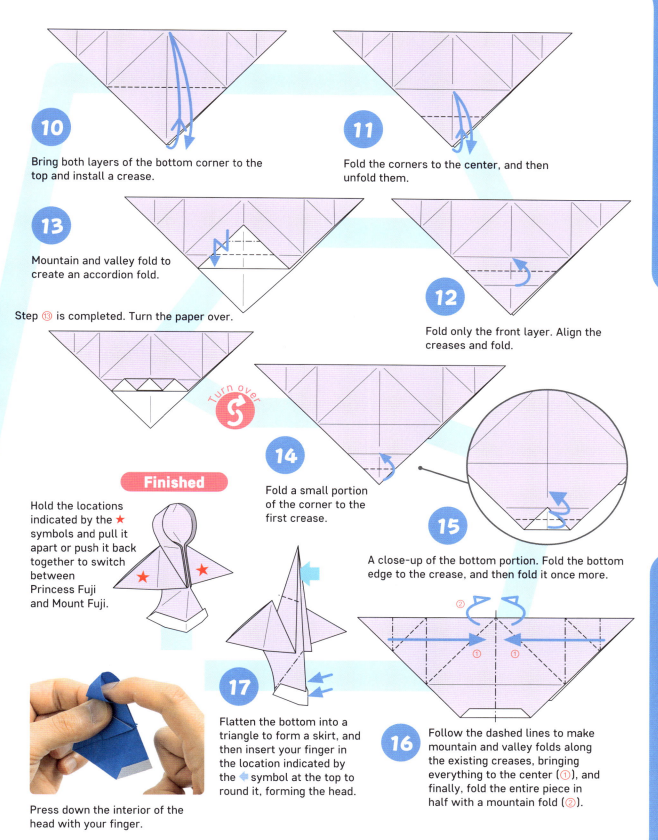

Amazing Magic Tricks 51

Magic Rising Chair

When you release your finger, it's like magic! The paper flips and a chair appears.

VIDEO
Type this URL into your browser:
tuttlepublishing.com/action-origami

[Snap!]

Slide the finger you're pressing with off the back edge!

Fold an 8-Row Precrease (1) (see page 142).

1 Fold the sides in to align with the second crease from the left.

2 Fold the right corners diagonally into narrow triangular flaps, with the creases starting at about ⅓ of the distance from the center of the right edge.

Turn over

Step ② is completed. Turn the paper over top to bottom.

3 Lift the right side to form the backrest. Also, stand up the legs of the chair by spreading the underlying flaps.

Finished

When playing, lay the chair down on its back. Swivel the flap indicated by the ★ symbol and hold it down with your finger before releasing the spring!

52   **Chapter 2**

Chapter 3 Otherworldly Origami

Lantern Ghost Sticking Out Its Tongue

This one-eyed ghost sticks its tongue out and pulls it back in. Even though it's a ghost, it's still kind of cute!

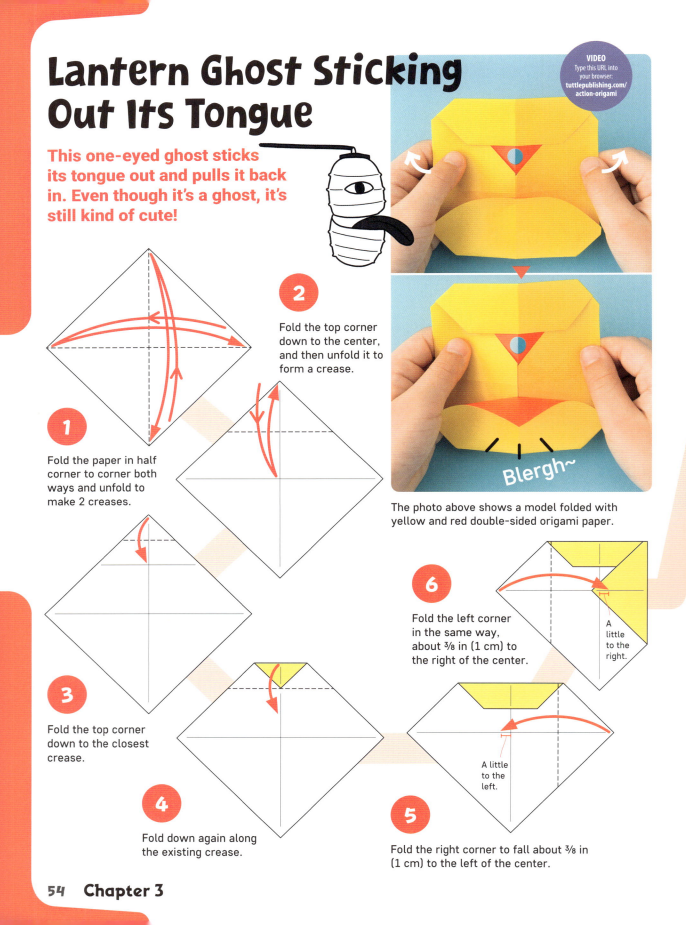

1 Fold the paper in half corner to corner both ways and unfold to make 2 creases.

2 Fold the top corner down to the center, and then unfold it to form a crease.

3 Fold the top corner down to the closest crease.

4 Fold down again along the existing crease.

5 Fold the right corner to fall about 3/8 in (1 cm) to the left of the center.

6 Fold the left corner in the same way, about 3/8 in (1 cm) to the right of the center.

The photo above shows a model folded with yellow and red double-sided origami paper.

54 Chapter 3

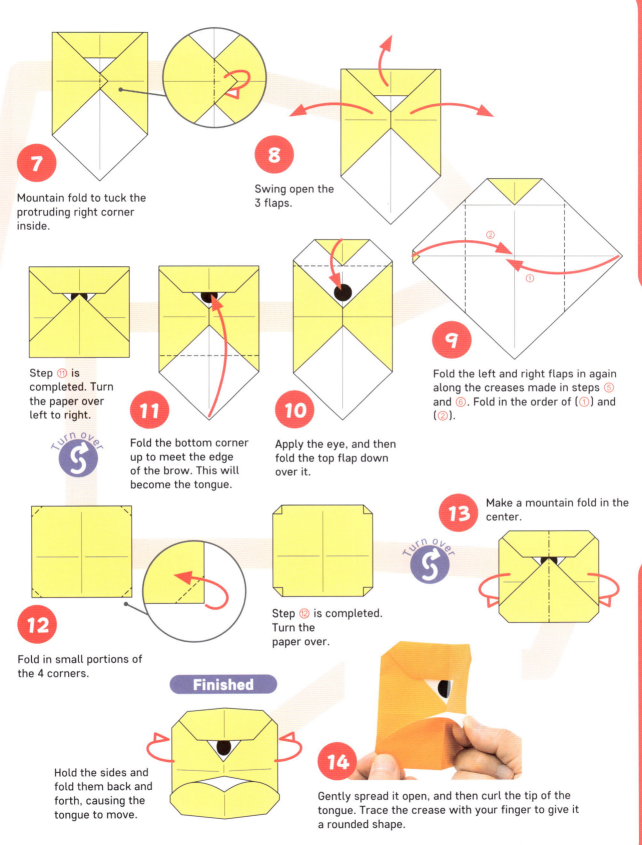

Otherworldly Origami 55

Chattering Skull

The skull clatters its jaw bone while chatting with you!

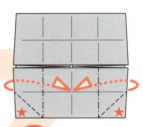

Hee hee hee!

Fold an 8-Row Precrease (1) (see page 142).

Rotate

2 Align the bottom corners with the crease and fold into triangles, then unfold.

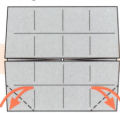

Step ③ in progress.

3 Lift the bottom flap slightly and fold both sides inward. The corners indicated by the ★ symbols will swivel behind the newly formed square topmost layer.

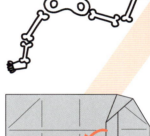

Step ⑥ in progress. Press down from the top to flatten it.

1 Orient the rectangle vertically and open it to this shape. Then, fold the top and bottom edges in to meet the center crease.

4 Fold the bottom up by 1 row.

Turn over

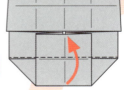

Step ④ is completed. Turn the paper over left to right.

5 Align the 4 corners with the creases, fold them into triangles, and then return them to their original positions.

6 Fold the top layer of both sides toward the center. Insert your fingers into the pockets that open, spread them out, and flatten them.

56 Chapter 3

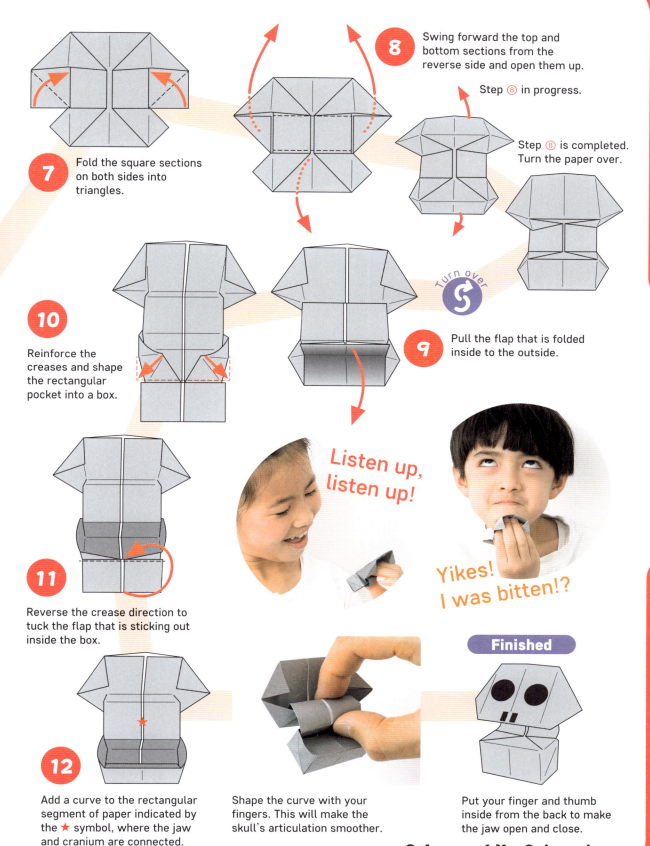

Otherworldly Origami 57

Gyrating Ghost

Watch the tail wobble around. It's a ghost, so it doesn't have legs!

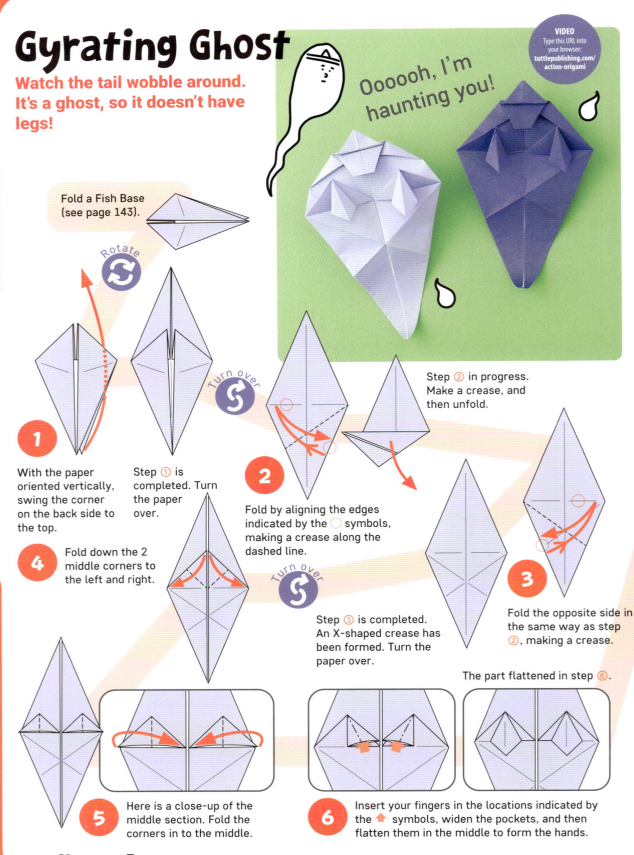

Ooooh, I'm haunting you!

VIDEO
Type this URL into your browser:
tuttlepublishing.com/action-origami

Fold a Fish Base (see page 143).

1 With the paper oriented vertically, swing the corner on the back side to the top.

Step ① is completed. Turn the paper over.

2 Fold by aligning the edges indicated by the ○ symbols, making a crease along the dashed line.

Step ② in progress. Make a crease, and then unfold.

3 Fold the opposite side in the same way as step ②, making a crease.

Step ③ is completed. An X-shaped crease has been formed. Turn the paper over.

4 Fold down the 2 middle corners to the left and right.

5 Here is a close-up of the middle section. Fold the corners in to the middle.

6 Insert your fingers in the locations indicated by the ⬆ symbols, widen the pockets, and then flatten them in the middle to form the hands.

The part flattened in step ⑥.

58 Chapter 3

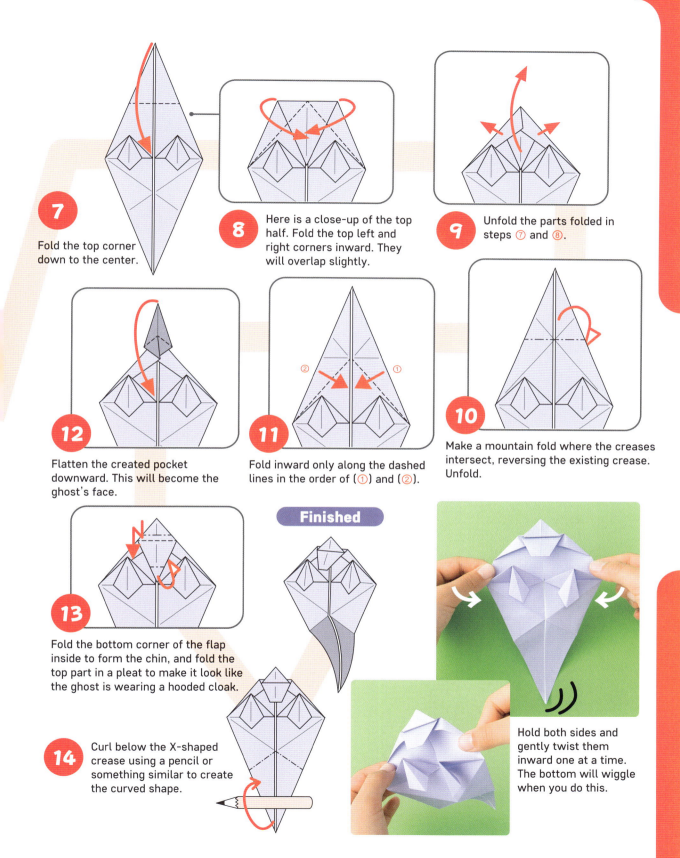

Staggering Zombie

This creepy character sticks out its arms and sways eerily back and forth.

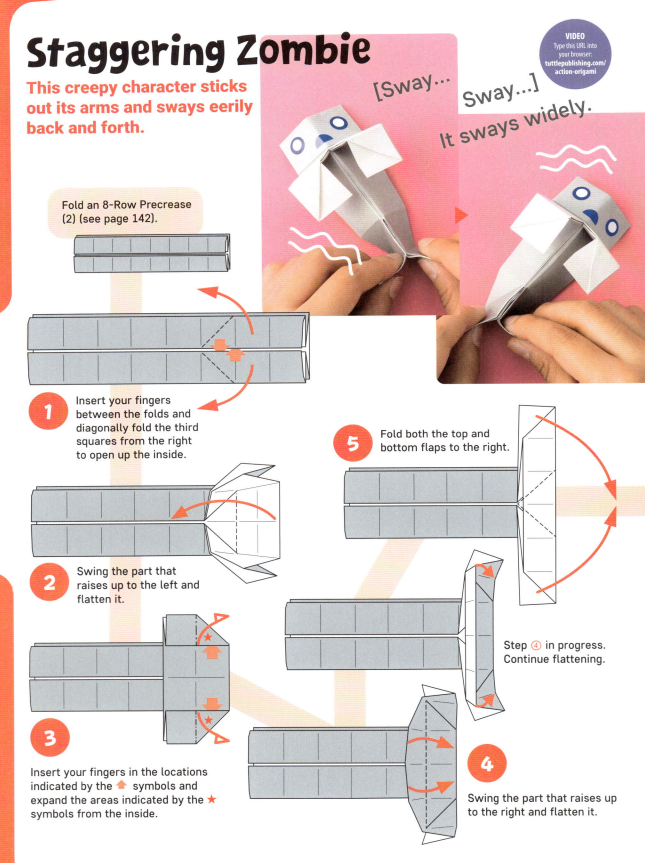

Fold an 8-Row Precrease (2) (see page 142).

1 Insert your fingers between the folds and diagonally fold the third squares from the right to open up the inside.

2 Swing the part that raises up to the left and flatten it.

3 Insert your fingers in the locations indicated by the ⬆ symbols and expand the areas indicated by the ★ symbols from the inside.

4 Swing the part that raises up to the right and flatten it.

Step ④ in progress. Continue flattening.

5 Fold both the top and bottom flaps to the right.

[Sway... Sway...] It sways widely.

VIDEO
Type this URL into your browser:
tuttlepublishing.com/action-origami

60 Chapter 3

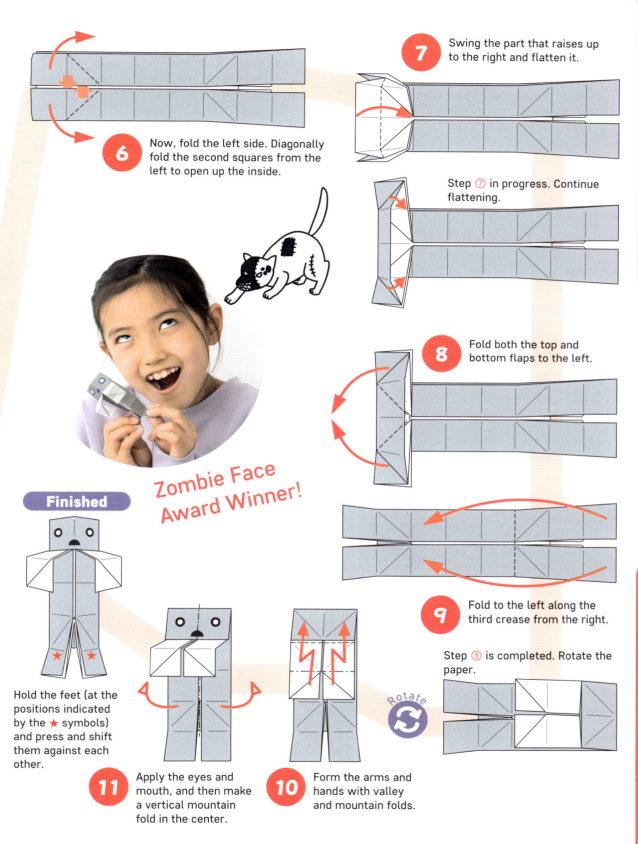

Otherworldly Origami 61

Flapping Bat

This model flaps its wings like the real thing, so cool! It is highly recommended as a Halloween decoration.

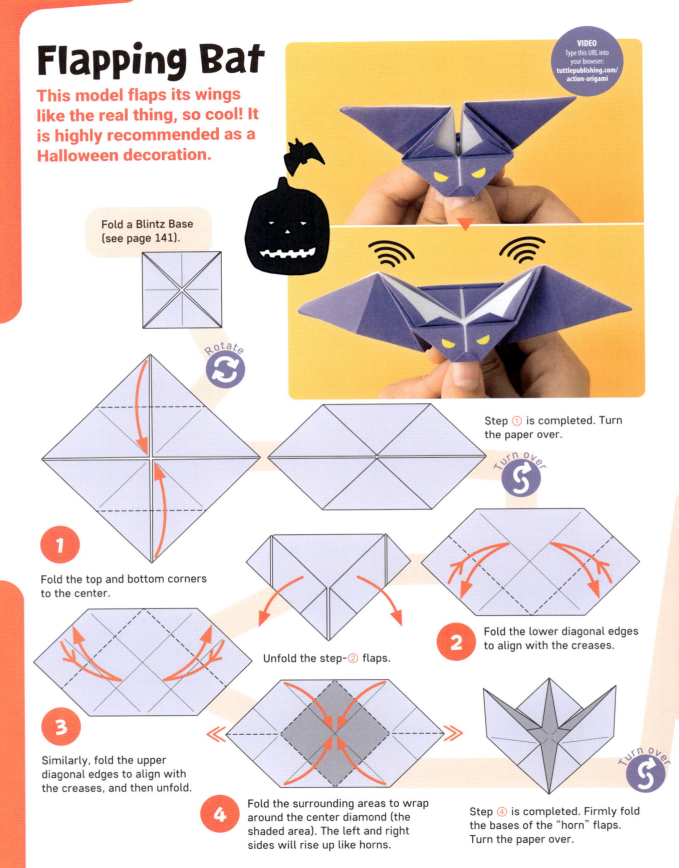

Fold a Blintz Base (see page 141).

1 Fold the top and bottom corners to the center.

2 Fold the lower diagonal edges to align with the creases.

Step ① is completed. Turn the paper over.

3 Similarly, fold the upper diagonal edges to align with the creases, and then unfold.

Unfold the step-② flaps.

4 Fold the surrounding areas to wrap around the center diamond (the shaded area). The left and right sides will rise up like horns.

Step ④ is completed. Firmly fold the bases of the "horn" flaps. Turn the paper over.

62   Chapter 3

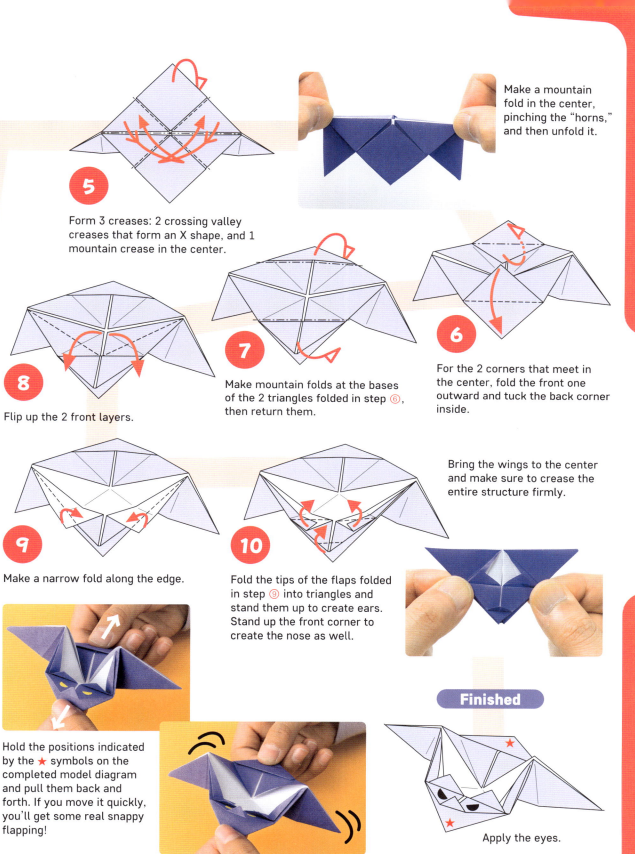

5
Form 3 creases: 2 crossing valley creases that form an X shape, and 1 mountain crease in the center.

Make a mountain fold in the center, pinching the "horns," and then unfold it.

6
For the 2 corners that meet in the center, fold the front one outward and tuck the back corner inside.

7
Make mountain folds at the bases of the 2 triangles folded in step ⑥, then return them.

8
Flip up the 2 front layers.

Bring the wings to the center and make sure to crease the entire structure firmly.

9
Make a narrow fold along the edge.

10
Fold the tips of the flaps folded in step ⑨ into triangles and stand them up to create ears. Stand up the front corner to create the nose as well.

Hold the positions indicated by the ★ symbols on the completed model diagram and pull them back and forth. If you move it quickly, you'll get some real snappy flapping!

Finished

Apply the eyes.

Otherworldly Origami 63

Kappa Eating a Fish

This creature is something more than just ordinary aquatic life. As a matter of fact, it's a *kappa* (river demon), and it swallows fish whole!

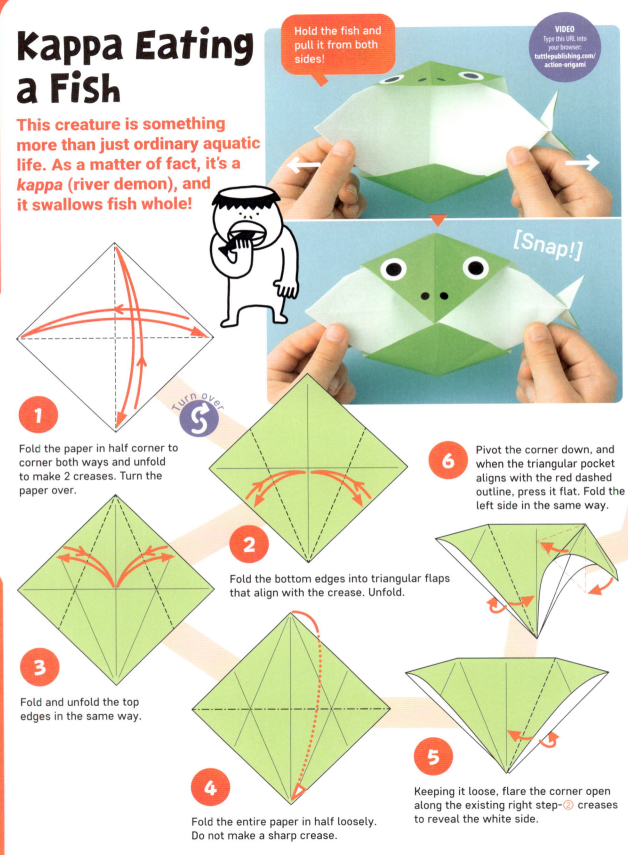

Hold the fish and pull it from both sides!

VIDEO Type this URL into your browser: tuttlepublishing.com/action-origami

[Snap!]

1 Fold the paper in half corner to corner both ways and unfold to make 2 creases. Turn the paper over.

Turn over

2 Fold the bottom edges into triangular flaps that align with the crease. Unfold.

3 Fold and unfold the top edges in the same way.

4 Fold the entire paper in half loosely. Do not make a sharp crease.

5 Keeping it loose, flare the corner open along the existing right step-② creases to reveal the white side.

6 Pivot the corner down, and when the triangular pocket aligns with the red dashed outline, press it flat. Fold the left side in the same way.

64   Chapter 3

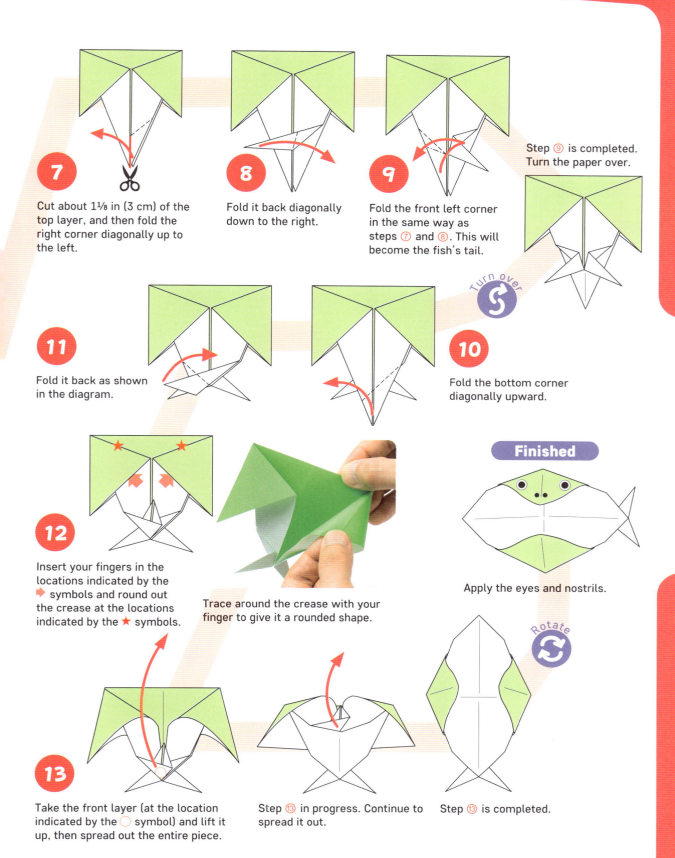

Otherworldly Origami

Rattling Lizard Cryptid

Is this the discovery of the century!? It looks like a lizard, but it's actually a mysterious cryptid.

[Rustle!]

[Rustle!]

VIDEO Type this URL into your browser: tuttlepublishing.com/action-origami

Fold an 8-Row Precrease (1) (see page 142).

Rotate

1 Orient the paper vertically, open it into this shape, and fold up from the bottom along the second crease.

2 This time, fold down from the top along the third crease.

Turn over

Step ② is completed. Turn the paper over.

3 Fold the 4 corners into triangles, and then unfold them to form creases.

Step ④ in progress.

4 Insert your fingers in the locations indicated by the ← symbols, and fold both sides to the center. The pockets that rise up should be opened and flattened.

66 **Chapter 3**

5 Swing the top and bottom flaps out from behind along the horizontal creases of the center squares, spreading the flaps open.

Step ⑤ in progress.

Step ⑤ is completed. Turn the paper over.

Step ⑥ is completed. Turn the paper over.

6 Fold the 4 corners inward, forming points at the top and bottom. These will become the head and tail.

7 Make mountain folds along the dashed lines on both sides, imparting boxiness to the shapes. Rotate the paper.

8 Gently curl the neck and the tip of tail.

Gently round it with your fingertips.

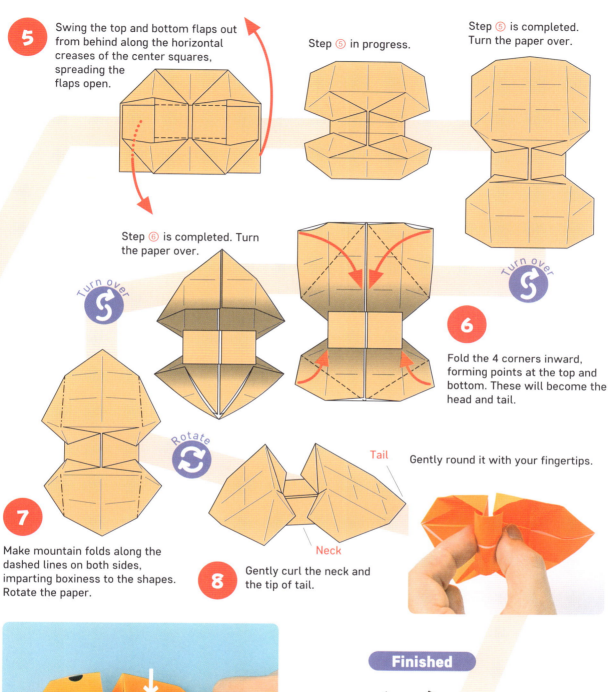

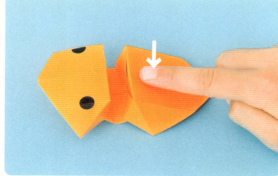

Lightly tap the raised part of the back from above to make it scoot forward.

Finished

Apply the eyes.

Otherworldly Origami 67

Jumping Sea Monster

Similar forms are often seen as gargoyles that decorate castle roofs. They are the guardian deities of the buildings!

VIDEO
Type this URL into your browser:
tuttlepublishing.com/action-origami

Fold an 8-Row Precrease (2) (see page 142).

[Boing Boing]

1 Insert your fingers between the folds and diagonally fold the fourth squares from the right to open up the inside.

2 Swing the part that raises up to the right and flatten it.

3 Insert your fingers in the locations indicated by the ⬆ symbols and expand the areas indicated by the ★ symbols from the inside.

4 Swivel the part that has risen to the left this time, and flatten it again.

Step ④ in progress.

Step ④ is completed. Turn the paper over.

5 Insert your fingers in the locations indicated by the ⬆ symbols and expand the areas indicated by the ★ symbols, folding in the top and bottom edges.

Turn over

68 Chapter 3

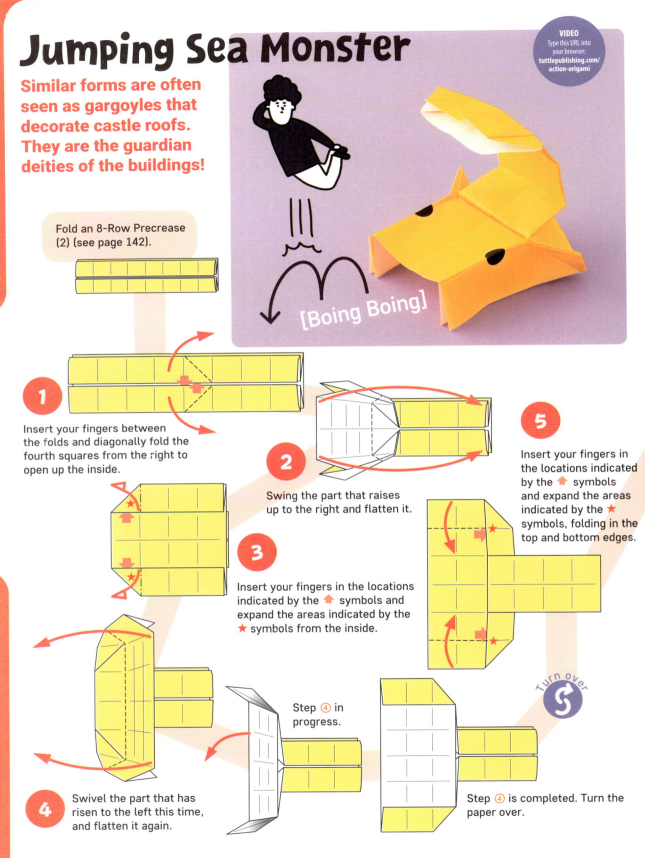

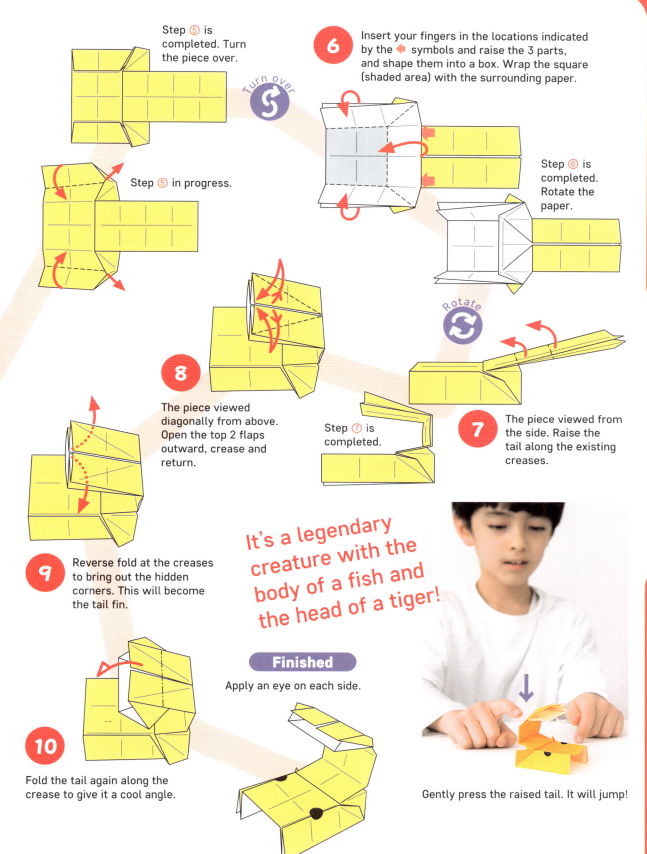

Step ⑤ is completed. Turn the piece over.

Step ⑤ in progress.

6 Insert your fingers in the locations indicated by the ← symbols and raise the 3 parts, and shape them into a box. Wrap the square (shaded area) with the surrounding paper.

Step ⑥ is completed. Rotate the paper.

8 The piece viewed diagonally from above. Open the top 2 flaps outward, crease and return.

Step ⑦ is completed.

7 The piece viewed from the side. Raise the tail along the existing creases.

9 Reverse fold at the creases to bring out the hidden corners. This will become the tail fin.

It's a legendary creature with the body of a fish and the head of a tiger!

Finished
Apply an eye on each side.

10 Fold the tail again along the crease to give it a cool angle.

Gently press the raised tail. It will jump!

Otherworldly Origami 69

Ninja Throwing a Star

This character quickly flicks its right hand as if throwing a *shuriken* (throwing star) at an enemy!

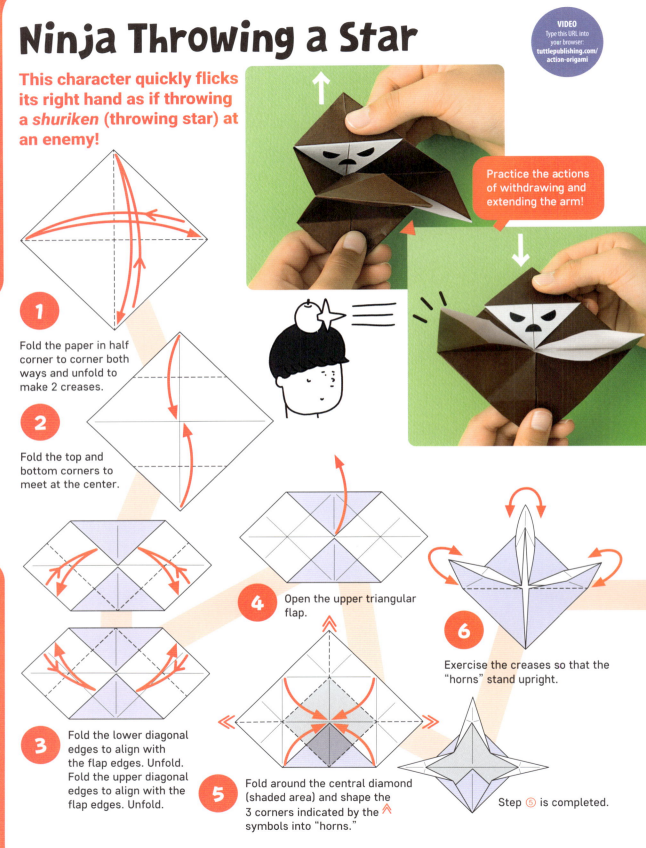

1 Fold the paper in half corner to corner both ways and unfold to make 2 creases.

2 Fold the top and bottom corners to meet at the center.

3 Fold the lower diagonal edges to align with the flap edges. Unfold. Fold the upper diagonal edges to align with the flap edges. Unfold.

4 Open the upper triangular flap.

5 Fold around the central diamond (shaded area) and shape the 3 corners indicated by the symbols into "horns."

6 Exercise the creases so that the "horns" stand upright.

Practice the actions of withdrawing and extending the arm!

Step ⑤ is completed.

70 Chapter 3

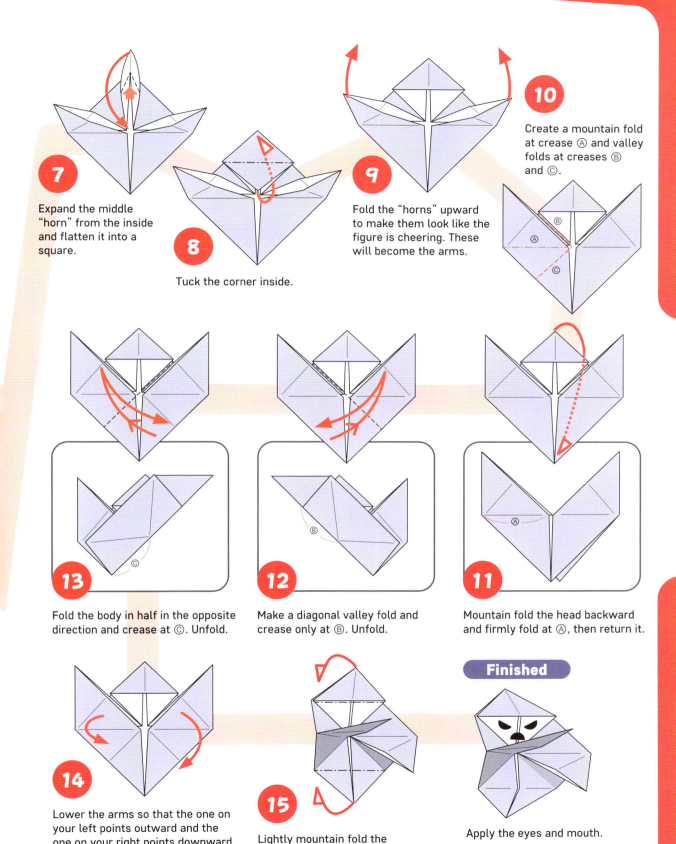

Otherworldly Origami 71

Slicing Samurai

"Kiai!" The samurai swings his sword down with grim determination.

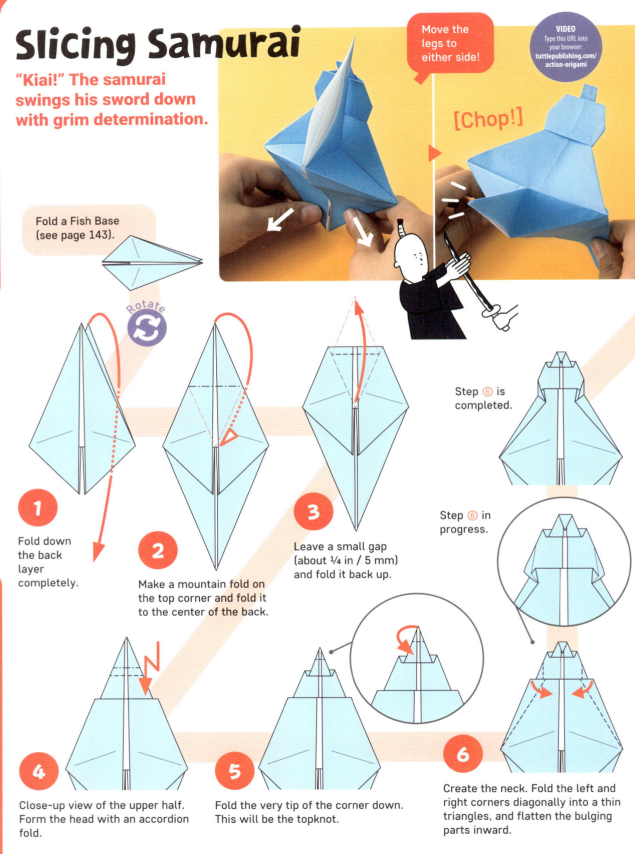

Fold a Fish Base (see page 143).

1 Fold down the back layer completely.

2 Make a mountain fold on the top corner and fold it to the center of the back.

3 Leave a small gap (about ¼ in / 5 mm) and fold it back up.

Step ⑥ is completed.

Step ⑥ in progress.

4 Close-up view of the upper half. Form the head with an accordion fold.

5 Fold the very tip of the corner down. This will be the topknot.

6 Create the neck. Fold the left and right corners diagonally into a thin triangles, and flatten the bulging parts inward.

72 Chapter 3

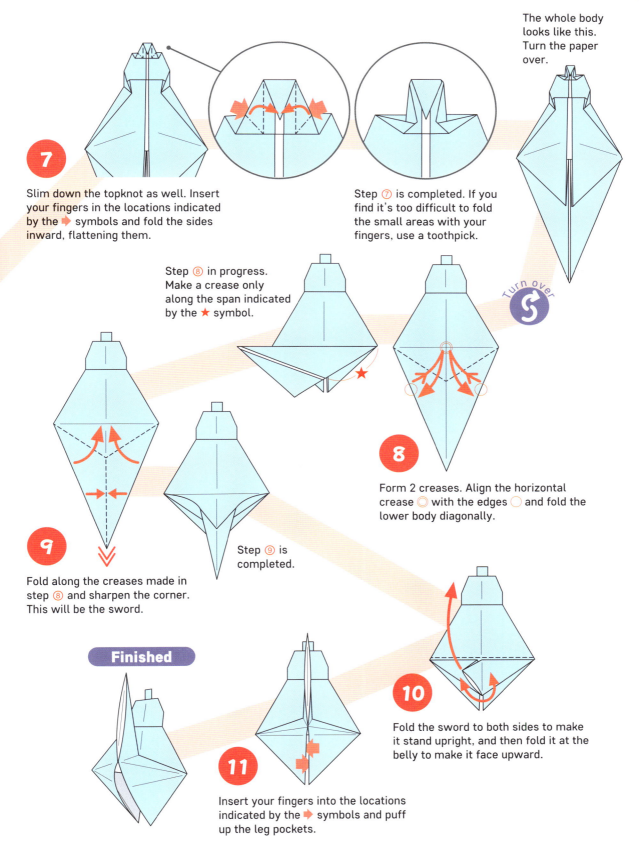

7

Slim down the topknot as well. Insert your fingers in the locations indicated by the ➡ symbols and fold the sides inward, flattening them.

Step ⑦ is completed. If you find it's too difficult to fold the small areas with your fingers, use a toothpick.

The whole body looks like this. Turn the paper over.

Step ⑧ in progress. Make a crease only along the span indicated by the ★ symbol.

8

Form 2 creases. Align the horizontal crease ◯ with the edges ◯ and fold the lower body diagonally.

9

Fold along the creases made in step ⑧ and sharpen the corner. This will be the sword.

Step ⑨ is completed.

10

Fold the sword to both sides to make it stand upright, and then fold it at the belly to make it face upward.

Finished

11

Insert your fingers into the locations indicated by the ➡ symbols and puff up the leg pockets.

Otherworldly Origami 73

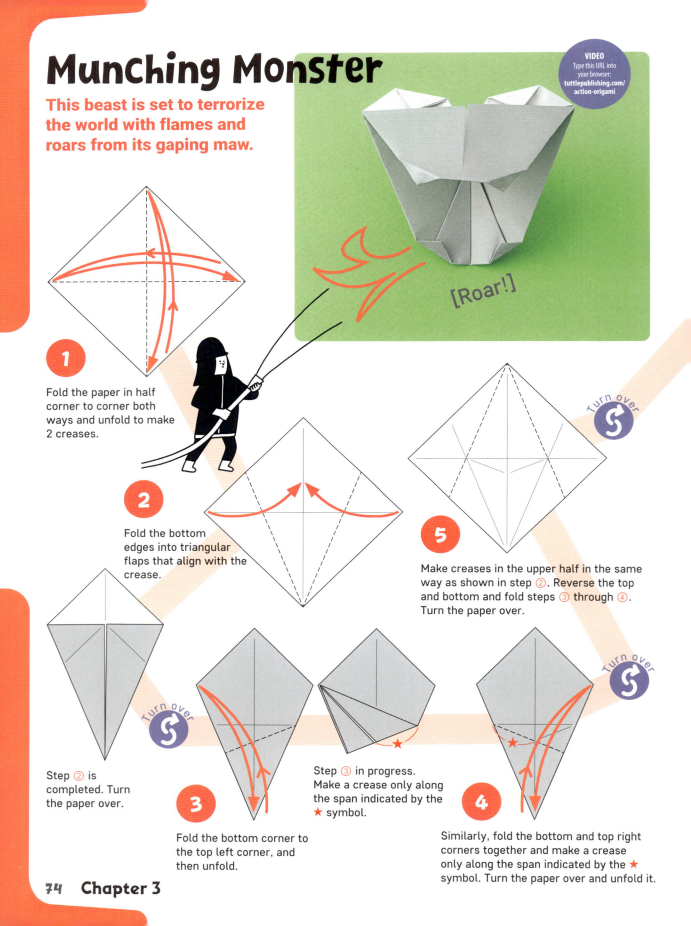

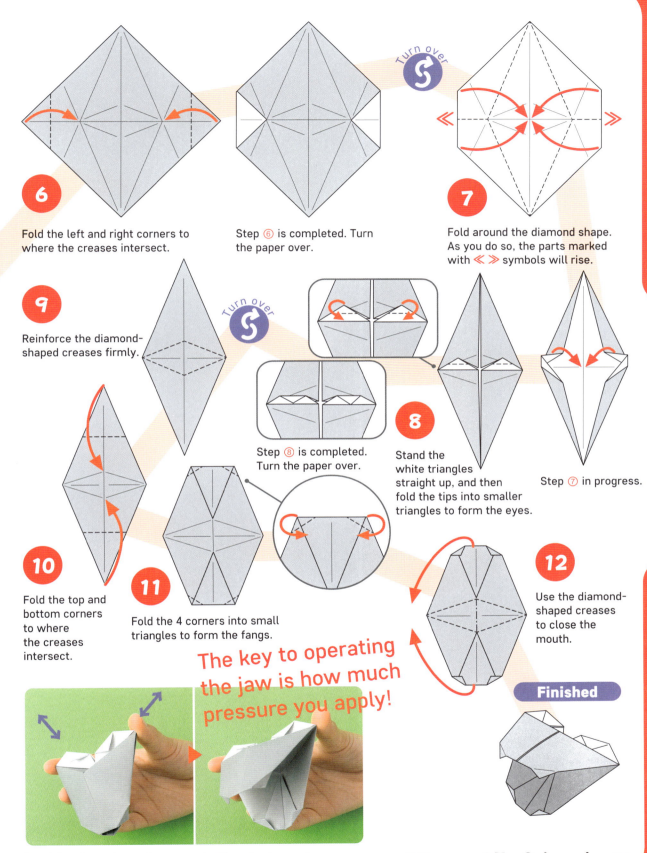

Otherworldly Origami 75

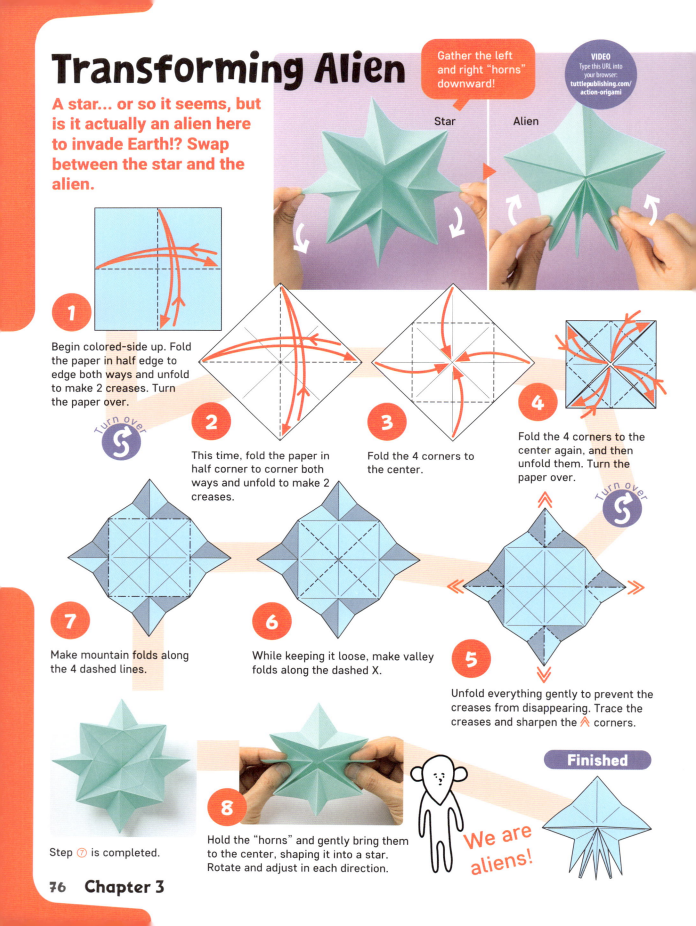

Chapter 4: Awesome Toys

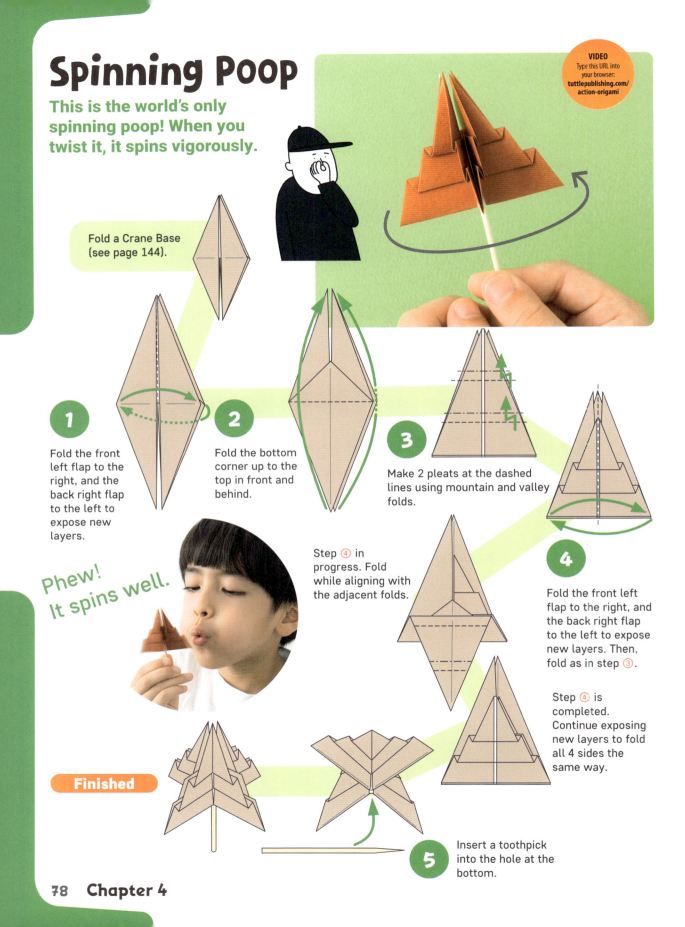

Self-Destruct Button (1)

Even though it's tempting to press it, I wouldn't risk it!

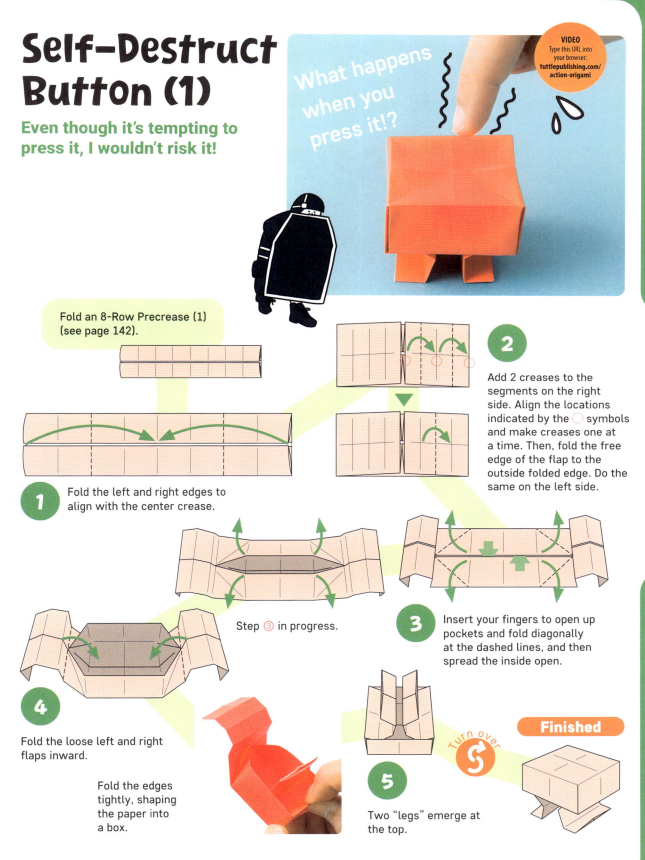

Awesome Toys

Self-Destruct Button (2)

This is a different button from the one on page 79, but it's just as dangerous and thrilling!

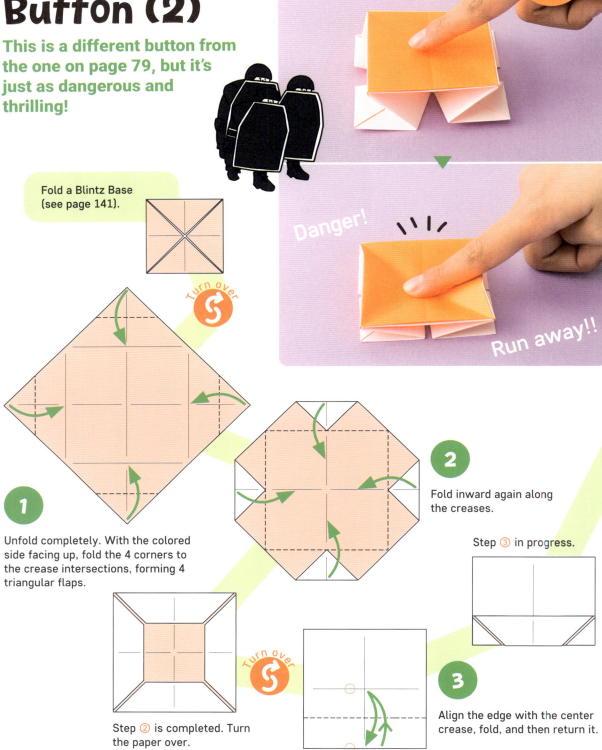

Fold a Blintz Base (see page 141).

1 Unfold completely. With the colored side facing up, fold the 4 corners to the crease intersections, forming 4 triangular flaps.

Step ② is completed. Turn the paper over.

2 Fold inward again along the creases.

Step ③ in progress.

3 Align the edge with the center crease, fold, and then return it.

80　Chapter 4

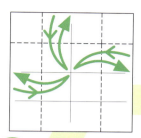

4 Do the same with the edges of the other 3 sides: fold and then return them.

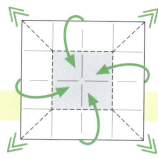

5 Fold the 4 edges inward. The corners will stand up like horns.

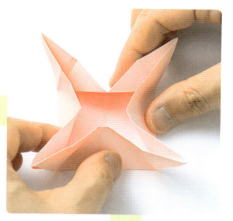

Fold the "horns" and their bases firmly so that they stand up straight.

Step ⑥ is completed.

Step ⑥ in progress.

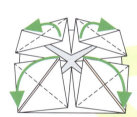

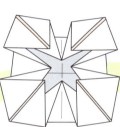

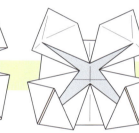

6 Insert your finger into the "horns" you created, expand them, and then press them toward the center.

7 Fold the 4 corners outward into triangles. These will become the springs of the button.

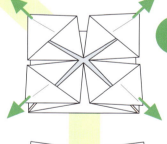

8 Gently pull and expand the springs.

Finished

Turn over

The parts expanded in step ⑧.

If it starts to lose tension, perform step ⑧ again and slightly stretch the springs to restore them.

Awesome Toys

Flexible Sword

It looks cool when you clash these swords. With this item, you might even defeat a monster... maybe?

Fold an 8-Row Precrease (2) (see page 142).

VIDEO
Type this URL into your browser:
tuttlepublishing.com/action-origami

It bends smoothly!

1 Unfold it entirely, place the colored side up, and then fold the right corners into triangular flaps that align with the center crease.

2 Fold the top and bottom edges to the center crease.

Step ② is completed. Turn the paper over.

3 Fold in the top and bottom edges again. Allow the hidden flaps to swing out from behind.

4 Fold the flaps exposed in step ③ to the center.

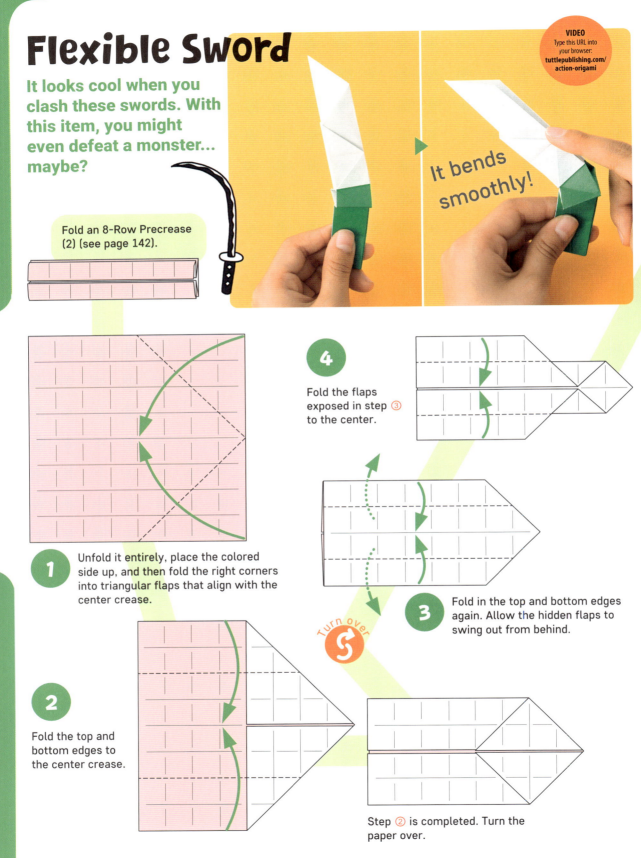

82 Chapter 4

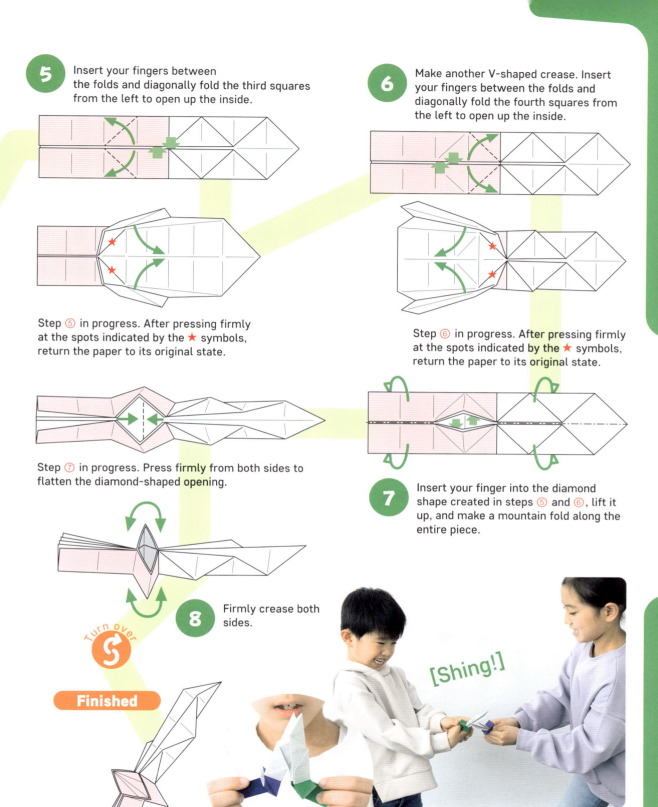

5 Insert your fingers between the folds and diagonally fold the third squares from the left to open up the inside.

Step ⑤ in progress. After pressing firmly at the spots indicated by the ★ symbols, return the paper to its original state.

6 Make another V-shaped crease. Insert your fingers between the folds and diagonally fold the fourth squares from the left to open up the inside.

Step ⑥ in progress. After pressing firmly at the spots indicated by the ★ symbols, return the paper to its original state.

Step ⑦ in progress. Press firmly from both sides to flatten the diamond-shaped opening.

7 Insert your finger into the diamond shape created in steps ⑤ and ⑥, lift it up, and make a mountain fold along the entire piece.

Turn over

8 Firmly crease both sides.

Finished

[Shing!]

The diamond shape acts as a spring, allowing the sword to bend.

Awesome Toys 83

Power Shovel Arm

A powerful shovel that looks like it could dig right into the ground. With its useful bucket, you could scoop up all the candy from a bowl, for instance!

VIDEO Type this URL into your browser: tuttlepublishing.com/action-origami

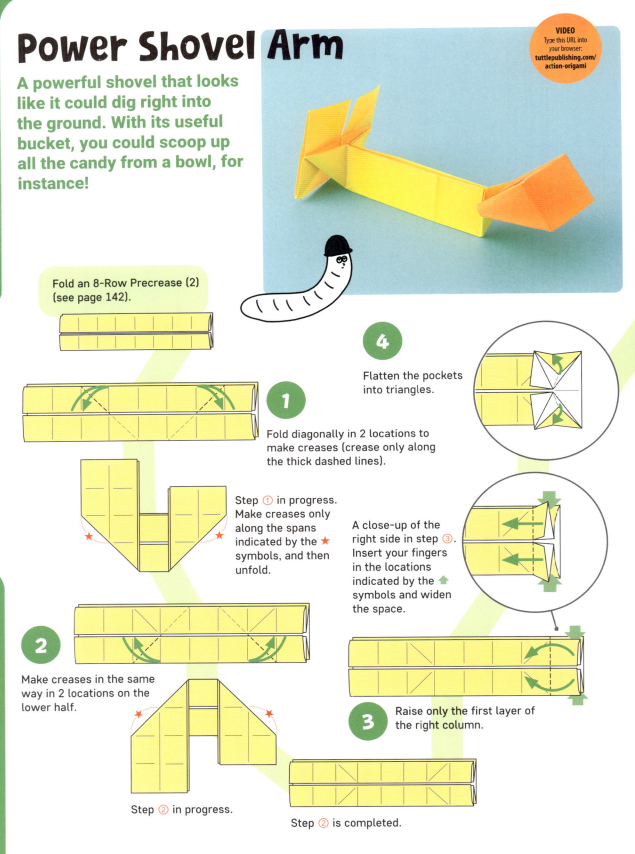

Fold an 8-Row Precrease (2) (see page 142).

1 Fold diagonally in 2 locations to make creases (crease only along the thick dashed lines).

Step ① in progress. Make creases only along the spans indicated by the ★ symbols, and then unfold.

2 Make creases in the same way in 2 locations on the lower half.

Step ② in progress.

Step ② is completed.

3 Raise only the first layer of the right column.

A close-up of the right side in step ③. Insert your fingers in the locations indicated by the ⬆ symbols and widen the space.

4 Flatten the pockets into triangles.

84 Chapter 4

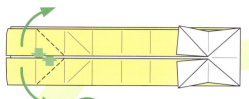
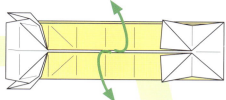

5 Fold the second column from the left diagonally at 2 spots, then open up the inside from the ⬆ symbols.

6 Pull open the flaps from the center.

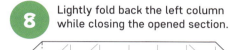

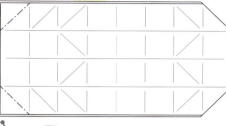

7 Fold the top and bottom corners on the left edge into triangles and tuck them inside.

8 Lightly fold back the left column while closing the opened section.

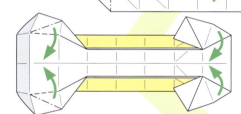
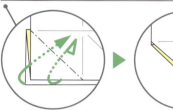

Step **8** in progress.

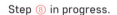

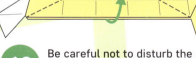
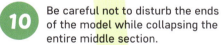

9 Raise the right square. This will become the handle.

10 Be careful not to disturb the ends of the model while collapsing the entire middle section.

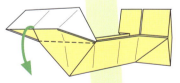

11 The view from the front left. Fold down the base of the shovel.

Finished

Come here, little candies!

When you open and close the handle's square, the arm moves up and down.

Hold the positions indicated by the ★ symbols to manipulate the arm.

Awesome Toys 85

Kickable Cleats

Kick around a ball with friends using folded origami soccer cleats.

Competing will fire you up!

VIDEO
Type this URL into your browser:
tuttlepublishing.com/
action-origami

Fold a Balloon Base (see page 143).

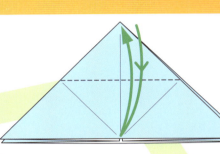

1 Fold the left and right corners of the uppermost layer up to the top and make creases. Unfold.

2 Fold the top down to the bottom and create a crease. Unfold.

3 Lift only the uppermost layer and align it with the top.

4 Align the corners that have risen on the sides with the bottom center, then fold and flatten them.

5 Fold the top corner down to the bottom.

Who will kick it first!?

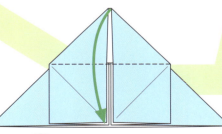

86   Chapter 4

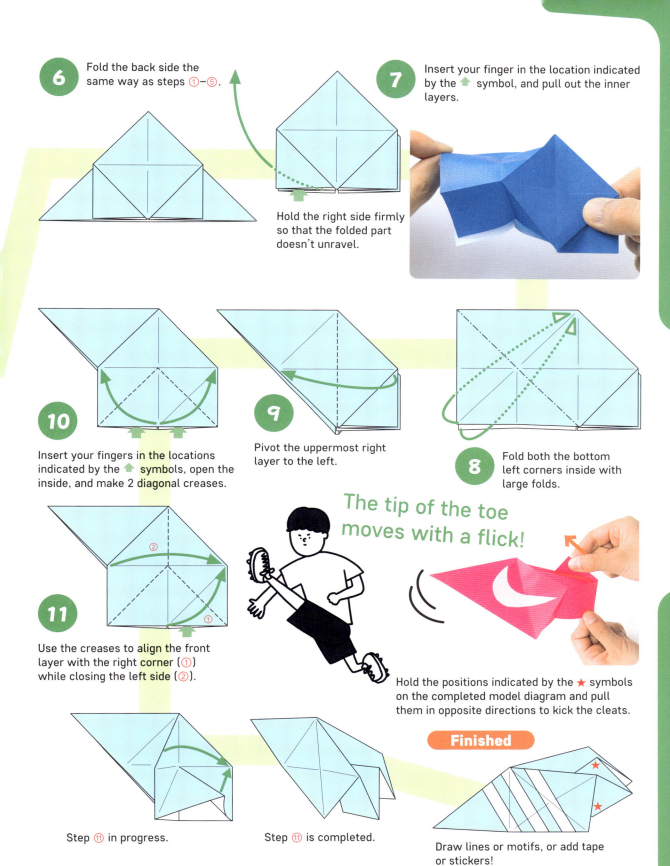

Awesome Toys 87

Catapult

It's up to you what to launch.
Send this or that flying away!

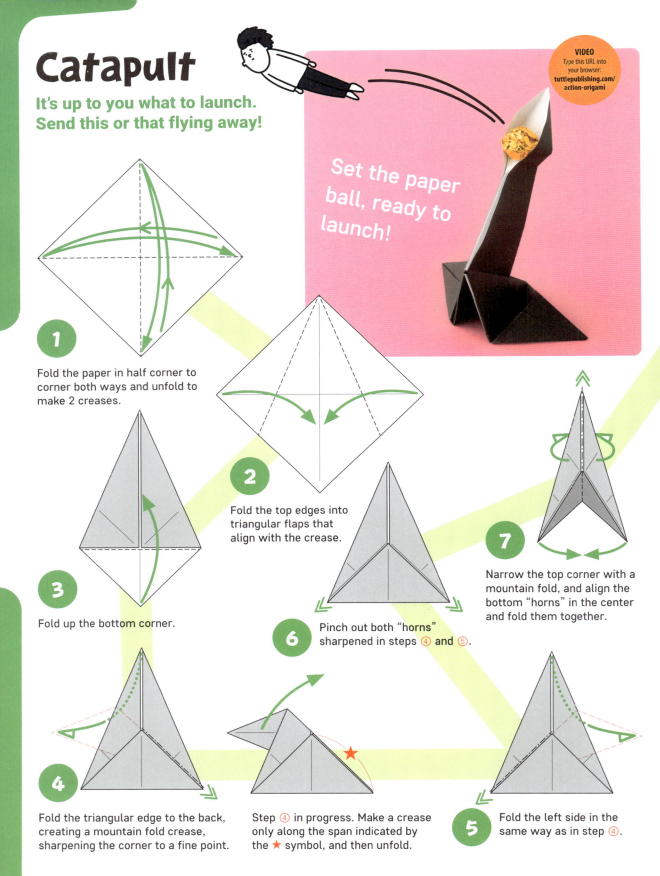

Set the paper ball, ready to launch!

VIDEO Type this URL into your browser: tuttlepublishing.com/ action-origami

1 Fold the paper in half corner to corner both ways and unfold to make 2 creases.

2 Fold the top edges into triangular flaps that align with the crease.

3 Fold up the bottom corner.

4 Fold the triangular edge to the back, creating a mountain fold crease, sharpening the corner to a fine point.

5 Fold the left side in the same way as in step ④.

6 Pinch out both "horns" sharpened in steps ④ and ⑤.

7 Narrow the top corner with a mountain fold, and align the bottom "horns" in the center and fold them together.

Step ④ in progress. Make a crease only along the span indicated by the ★ symbol, and then unfold.

88   Chapter 4

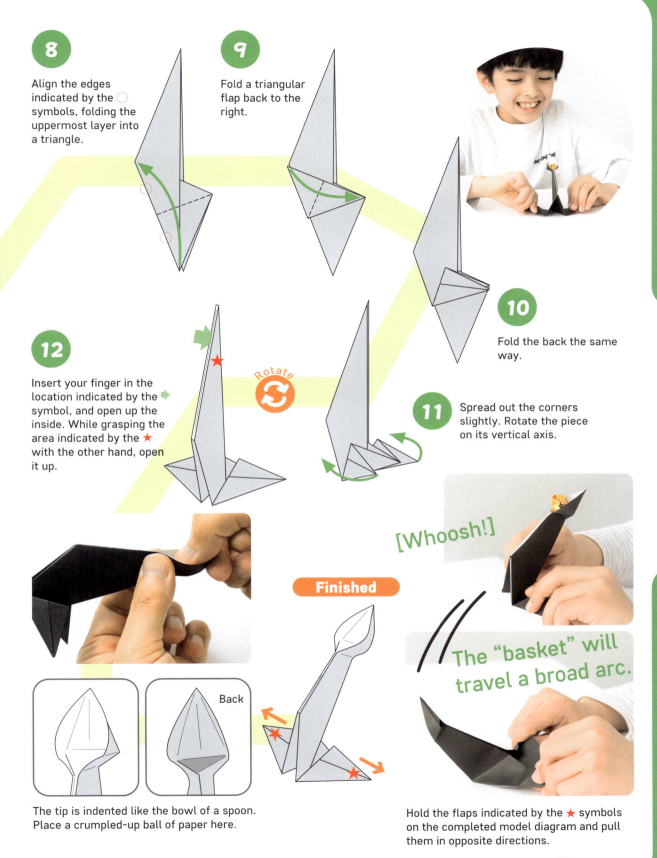

Spinning Shuriken

It's a new type of ninja star that cartwheels across a surface. The protruding triangular spikes look dangerous!

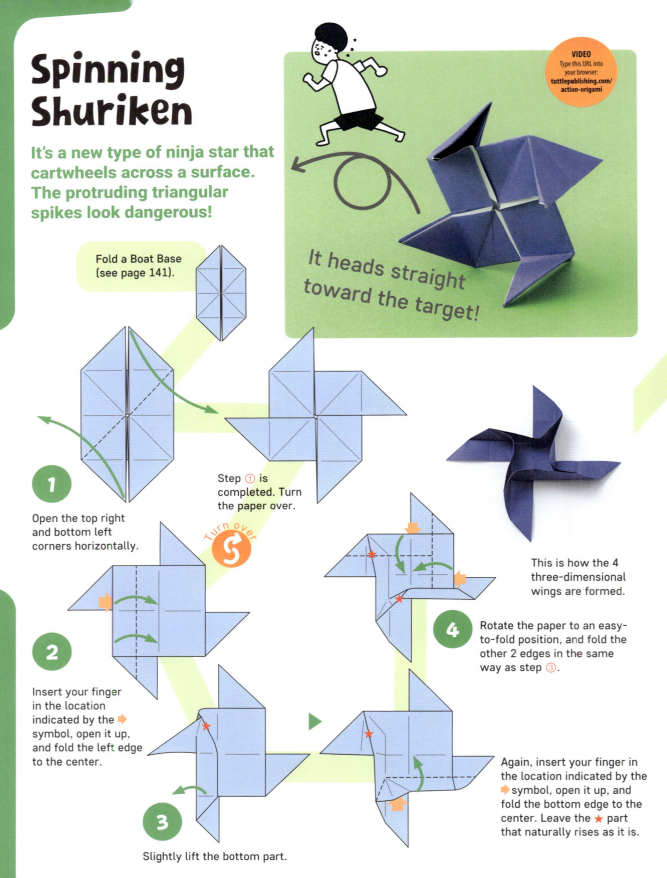

It heads straight toward the target!

VIDEO Type this URL into your browser: tuttlepublishing.com/action-origami

Fold a Boat Base (see page 141).

1 Open the top right and bottom left corners horizontally.

Step ① is completed. Turn the paper over.

2 Insert your finger in the location indicated by the ➡ symbol, open it up, and fold the left edge to the center.

3 Slightly lift the bottom part.

This is how the 4 three-dimensional wings are formed.

4 Rotate the paper to an easy-to-fold position, and fold the other 2 edges in the same way as step ③.

Again, insert your finger in the location indicated by the ➡ symbol, open it up, and fold the bottom edge to the center. Leave the ★ part that naturally rises as it is.

Chapter 4

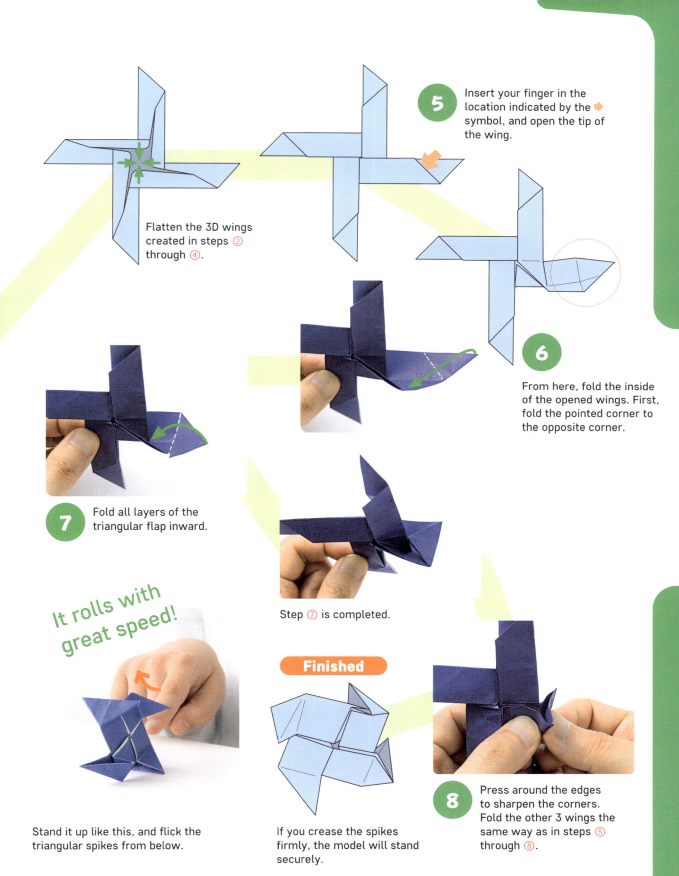

Awesome Toys

Spinning Shooting Star

It twirls around as it slides. Are you ready to make a wish!?

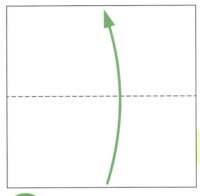

Just release the finger you're holding it with!

VIDEO
Type this URL into your browser:
tuttlepublishing.com/action-origami

1 Fold the paper in half, bottom edge to top.

2 Fold it in half again.

3 Fold the paper in half corner to corner both ways and unfold to make 2 creases.

4 Fold the paper in half edge to edge both ways and unfold to make 2 creases.

Step ③ is completed. Turn the paper over.

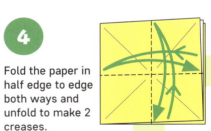

5 Pinch the corners indicated by the ⌃ symbols to sharpen them, making the center rise like a mountain.

Step ⑤ is completed. Press in at the locations indicated by the arrow marks and shape it into a star.

Finished

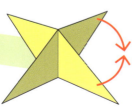

Hold the 2 wings together and launch it from a raised location, like a desk or table.

92 **Chapter 4**

Tree-Go-Round

Blow on it through a straw, and the tree will spin like a merry-go-round.

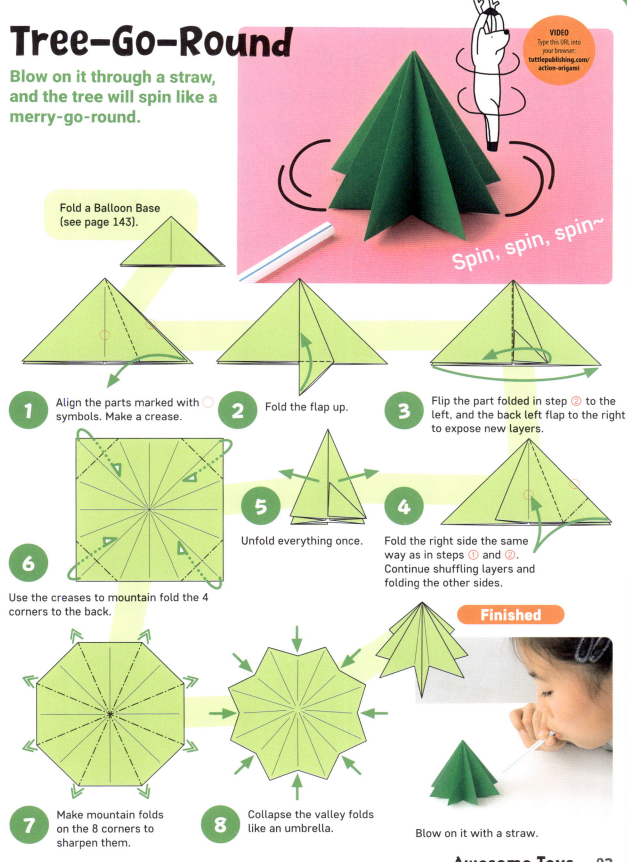

Fold a Balloon Base (see page 143).

1 Align the parts marked with ○ symbols. Make a crease.

2 Fold the flap up.

3 Flip the part folded in step ② to the left, and the back left flap to the right to expose new layers.

4 Fold the right side the same way as in steps ① and ②. Continue shuffling layers and folding the other sides.

5 Unfold everything once.

6 Use the creases to mountain fold the 4 corners to the back.

7 Make mountain folds on the 8 corners to sharpen them.

8 Collapse the valley folds like an umbrella.

Finished

Blow on it with a straw.

Awesome Toys 93

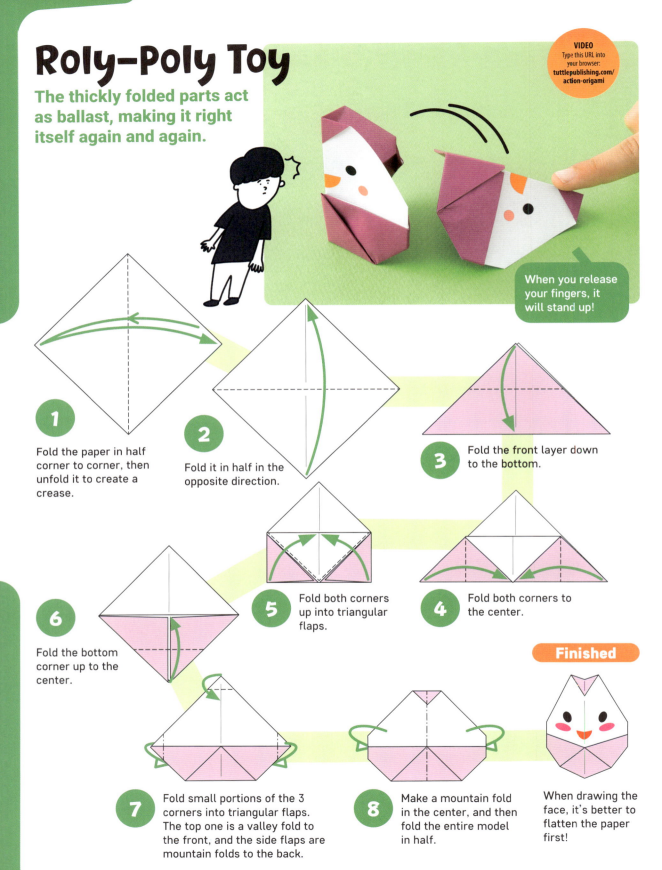

Jumping Airplane

This is a lively, gliding airplane that jumps and scoots! Have a speed and distance contest with your friends!

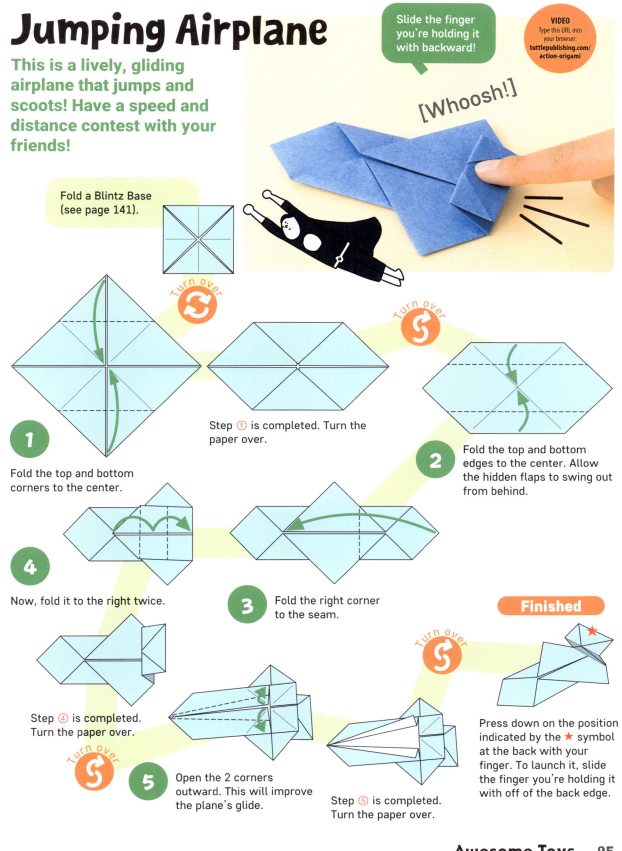

Awesome Toys　95

Spinning Propeller

The slightly angled wings are key! This gizmo spins gracefully while falling.

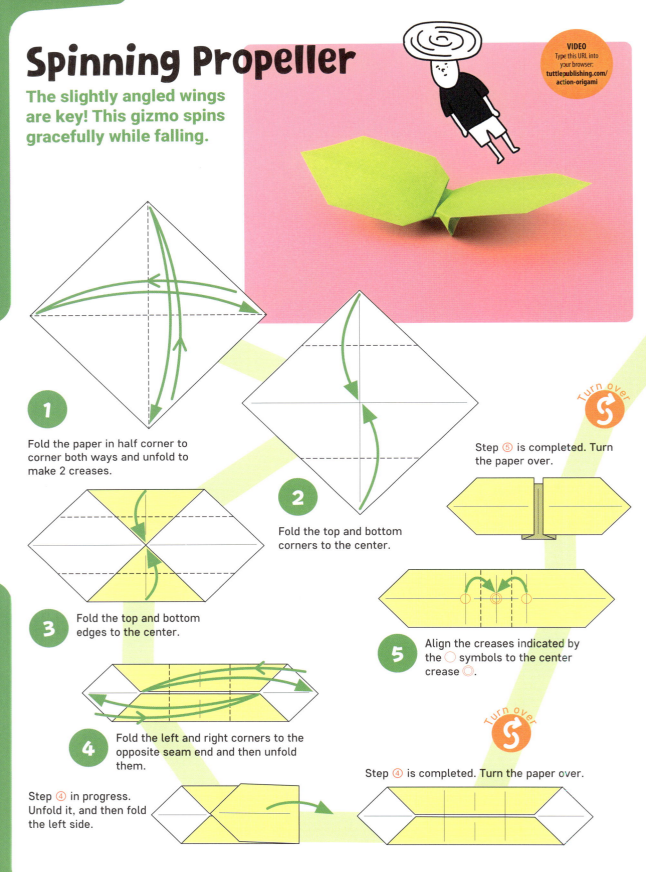

VIDEO Type this URL into your browser: tuttlepublishing.com/action-origami

1 Fold the paper in half corner to corner both ways and unfold to make 2 creases.

2 Fold the top and bottom corners to the center.

3 Fold the top and bottom edges to the center.

4 Fold the left and right corners to the opposite seam end and then unfold them.

Step ④ in progress. Unfold it, and then fold the left side.

Step ④ is completed. Turn the paper over.

5 Align the creases indicated by the ○ symbols to the center crease ◎.

Step ⑤ is completed. Turn the paper over.

96　Chapter 4

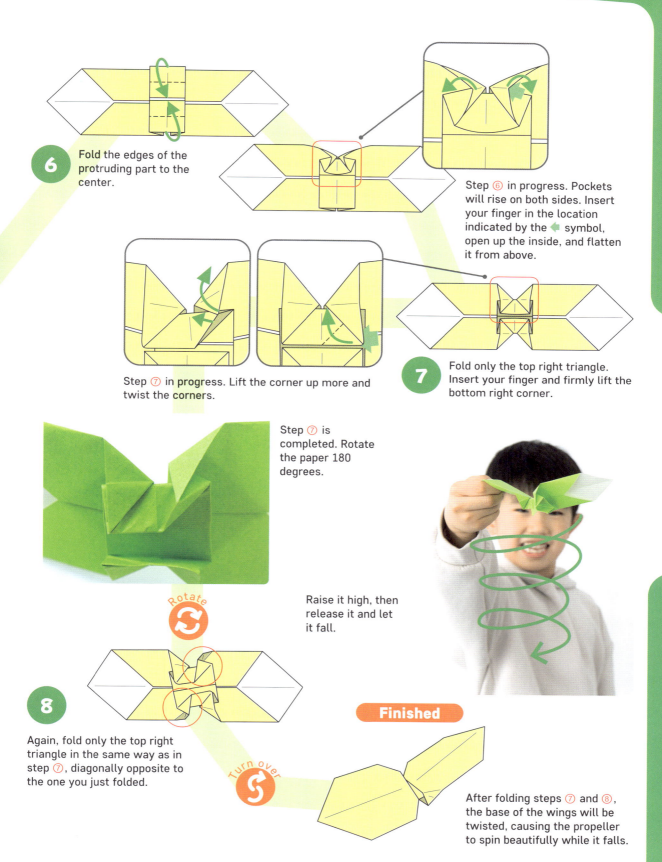

6 Fold the edges of the protruding part to the center.

Step ⑥ in progress. Pockets will rise on both sides. Insert your finger in the location indicated by the ← symbol, open up the inside, and flatten it from above.

7 Fold only the top right triangle. Insert your finger and firmly lift the bottom right corner.

Step ⑦ in progress. Lift the corner up more and twist the corners.

Step ⑦ is completed. Rotate the paper 180 degrees.

Raise it high, then release it and let it fall.

8 Again, fold only the top right triangle in the same way as in step ⑦, diagonally opposite to the one you just folded.

Finished

After folding steps ⑦ and ⑧, the base of the wings will be twisted, causing the propeller to spin beautifully while it falls.

Awesome Toys

Mount Fuji Airplane

Amazing! Japan's tallest mountain has been reimagined as an airplane. Fly it and feel like you're on top of the world!

It flies well even in the shape of a mountain!

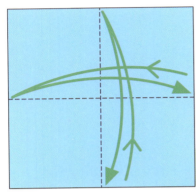

1 Fold the paper in half edge to edge both ways and unfold to make 2 creases.

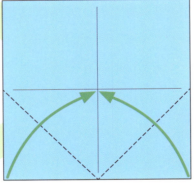

2 Fold the bottom corners up to the center.

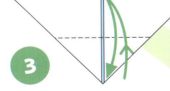

3 Fold the bottom corner up to the center, and then unfold it to create a crease.

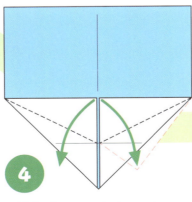

4 Fold the 2 corners in the center back along lines running from the step-③ crease to the outside corners so that the tips stick out.

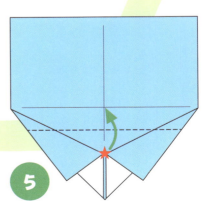

5 Fold the lower portion up so that the top of the seam (indicated by the ★ symbol) aligns with the intersection of the creases.

98 Chapter 4

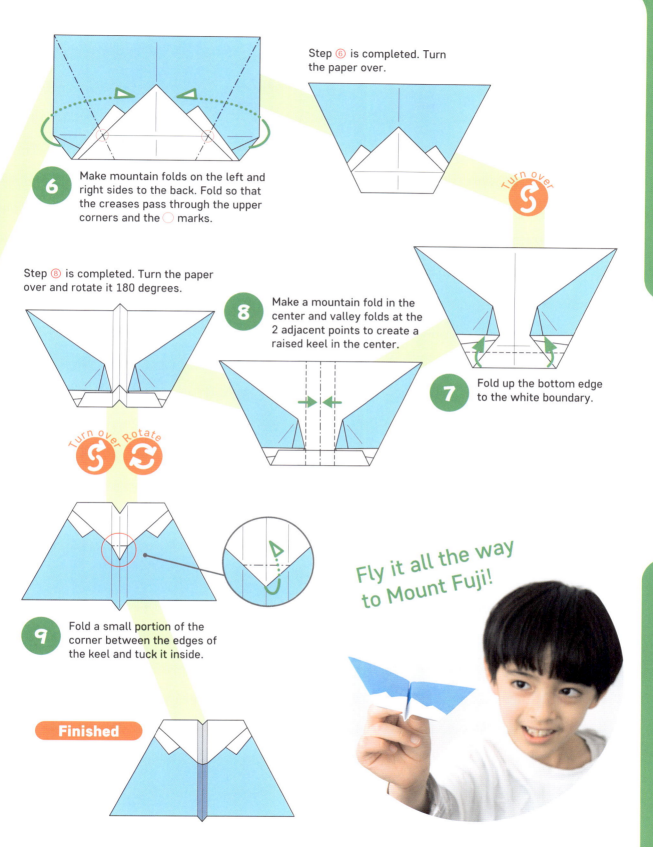

Whale Airplane

With its big mouth open wide, the whale glides through the sky!

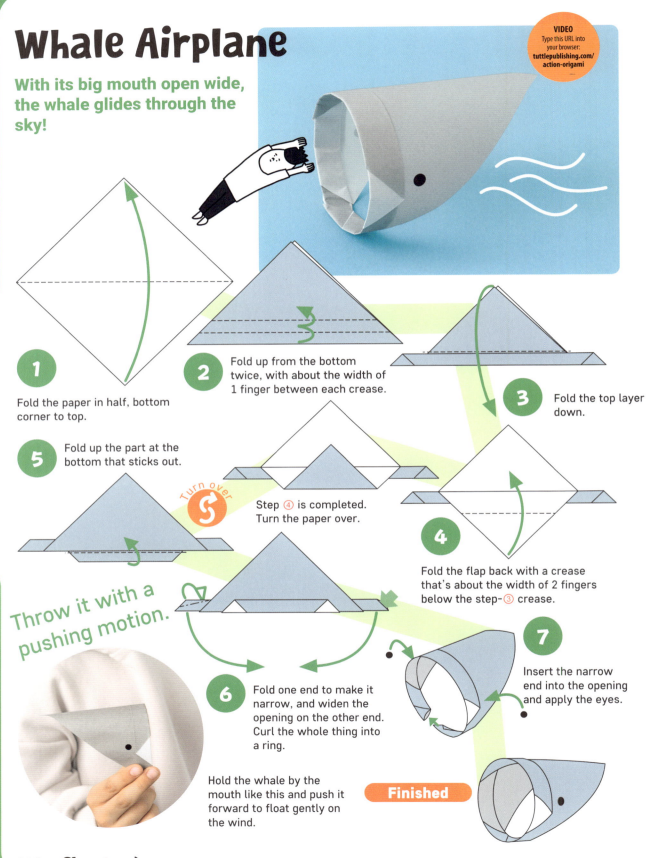

1. Fold the paper in half, bottom corner to top.
2. Fold up from the bottom twice, with about the width of 1 finger between each crease.
3. Fold the top layer down.
4. Fold the flap back with a crease that's about the width of 2 fingers below the step-③ crease.

Step ④ is completed. Turn the paper over.

5. Fold up the part at the bottom that sticks out.
6. Fold one end to make it narrow, and widen the opening on the other end. Curl the whole thing into a ring.

Hold the whale by the mouth like this and push it forward to float gently on the wind.

Throw it with a pushing motion.

7. Insert the narrow end into the opening and apply the eyes.

Finished

100 Chapter 4

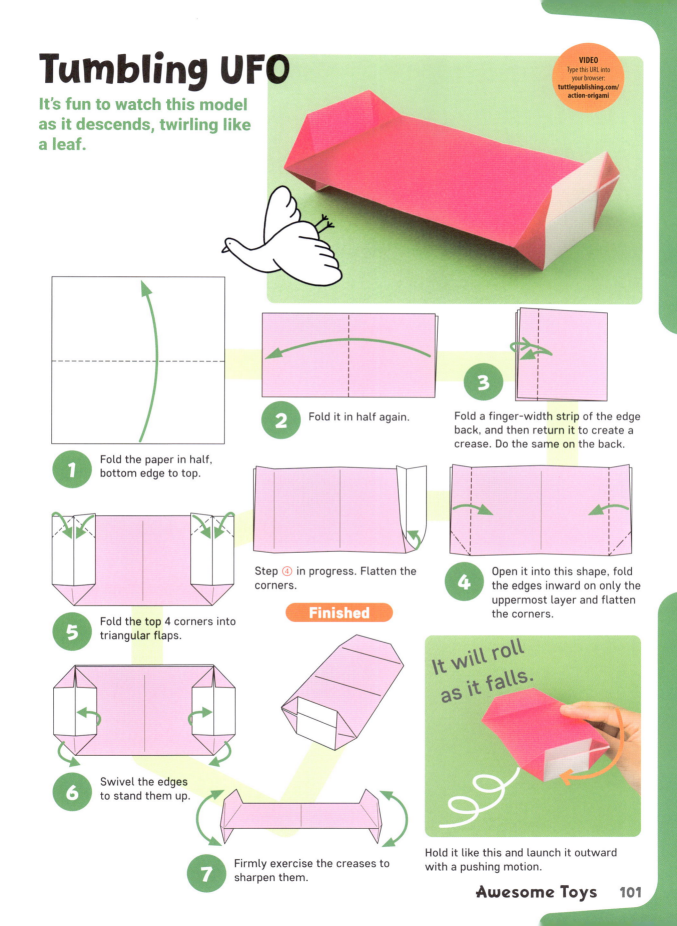

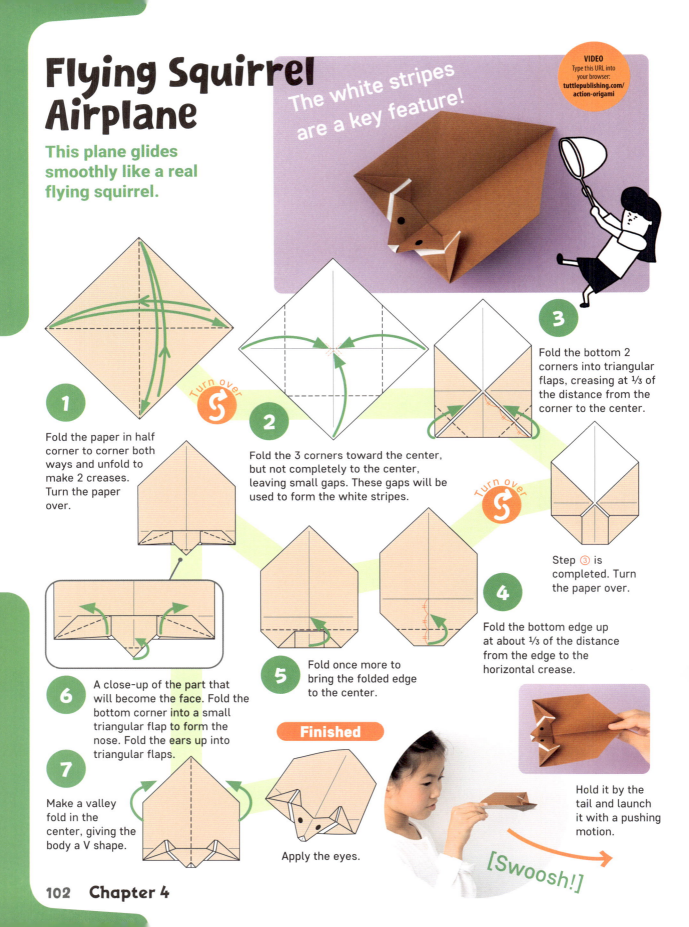

Chapter 5 Cute Chibi Animals

Monkey Playing Cymbals

A delightful toy monkey clashing cymbals in its hands. Have you seen one before?

VIDEO
Type this URL into your browser:
tuttlepublishing.com/action-origami

Fold a Boat Base (see page 141).

1 Firmly fold along the dashed lines and stand the 4 corners up.

2 Insert your fingers in the locations indicated by the ➡ symbols, open up the inside, and flatten each corner into a square. Do the same on the left side.

Step ② in progress.

Step ② is completed. Turn the paper over.

Turn over

3 Fold out the inside corners of the top and bottom squares. For the bottom square, make the crease and then return it.

4 Fold in a small portion of the top corner and make 2 valley folds with the bottom corner, rolling it.

5 Make mountain folds with the remaining 2 corners, tucking them inside.

104   Chapter 5

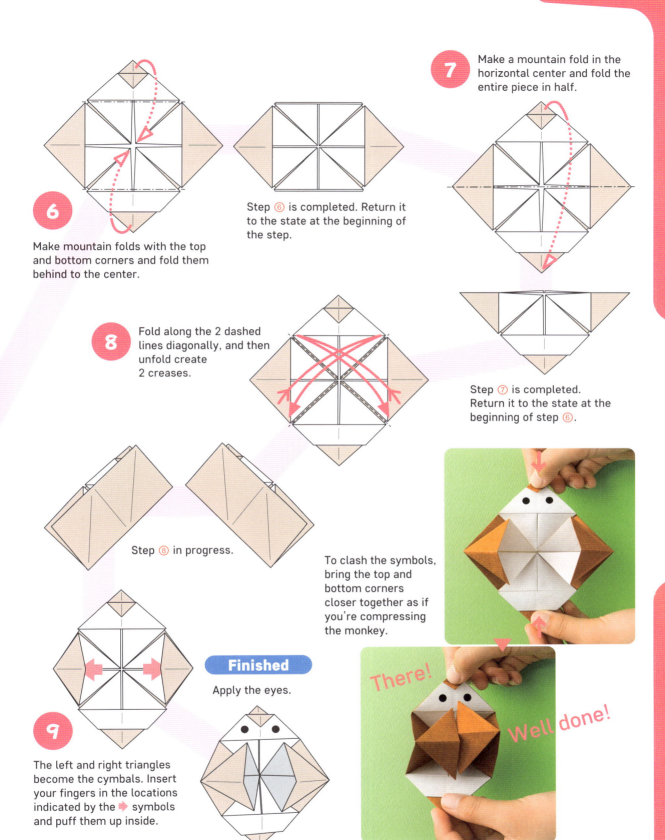

6 Make mountain folds with the top and bottom corners and fold them behind to the center.

Step ⑥ is completed. Return it to the state at the beginning of the step.

7 Make a mountain fold in the horizontal center and fold the entire piece in half.

Step ⑦ is completed. Return it to the state at the beginning of step ⑥.

8 Fold along the 2 dashed lines diagonally, and then unfold create 2 creases.

Step ⑧ in progress.

To clash the symbols, bring the top and bottom corners closer together as if you're compressing the monkey.

9 The left and right triangles become the cymbals. Insert your fingers in the locations indicated by the ➡ symbols and puff them up inside.

Finished

Apply the eyes.

There! Well done!

Cute Chibi Animals   105

Jumping Caterpillar

Using the spring power created by folded paper, this model will bounce and fly high. You can have a jumping competition too!

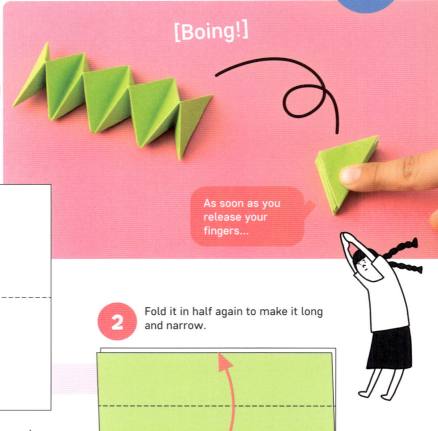

1 Fold the paper in half, bottom edge to top.

2 Fold it in half again to make it long and narrow.

3 Fold it in half horizontally and unfold to create a crease.

Turn over

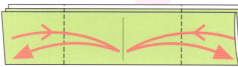

4 Fold the left and right edges to the center and unfold to make creases.

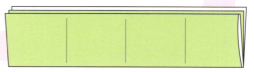

Step ④ is completed. Four square segments have been created. Turn the paper over left to right.

106   Chapter 5

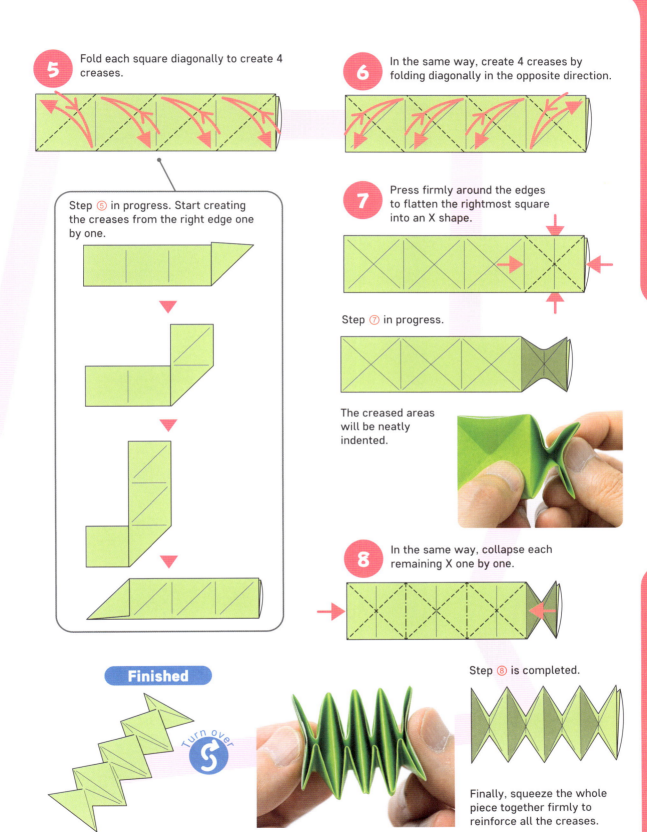

Charging Wild Boar & Rhino

Let's make them charge and snort. Make way!

◆ Rhinoceros

[Rumble, rumble, rumble!]

VIDEO Type this URL into your browser: tuttlepublishing.com/action-origami

Fold the Kickable Cleats (see page 86).

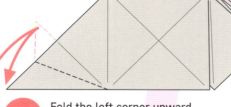

1 Outside reverse fold the left corner to form the nose. The outward fold is a bit tricky, so let's go through it step by step, starting with step ②.

2 Fold the left corner upward diagonally and then unfold it, making just a crease first.

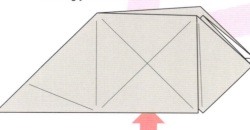

3 To make it easier to fold, insert your hand in the location indicated by the ⬆ symbol, and slightly open the inside.

4 This is a view from the nose side. Use the crease from step ② to flip the tip inside out.

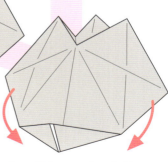

Step ④ is completed. Close up the sides to flatten the piece.

Finished

Apply the eyes.

108 Chapter 5

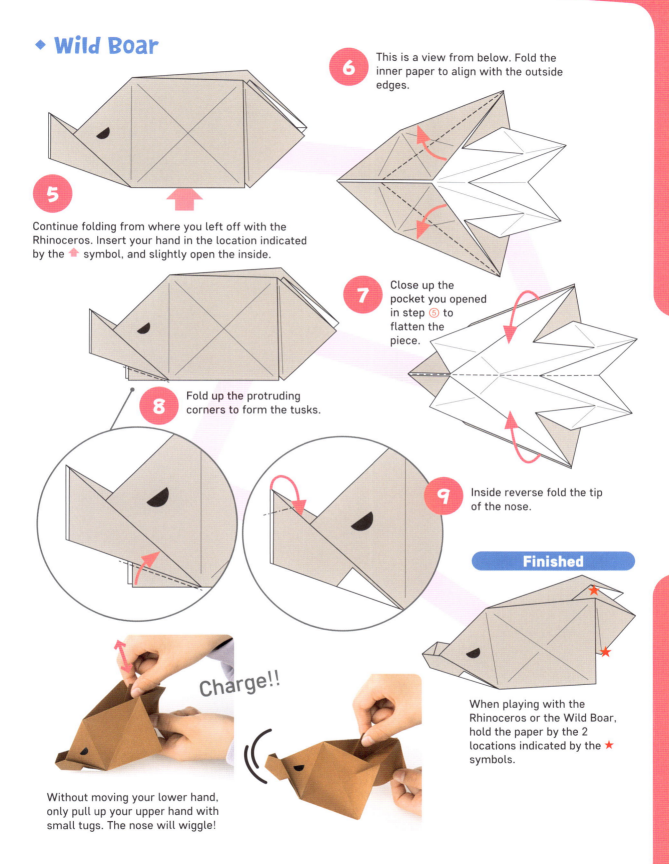

Headstand Penguin

This model is basically the opposite of the Roly-Poly Toy (page 94). This penguin will do a headstand with a twist!

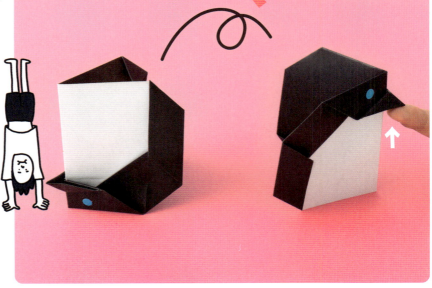

Flip it from below the beak!

VIDEO
Type this URL into your browser:
tuttlepublishing.com/action-origami

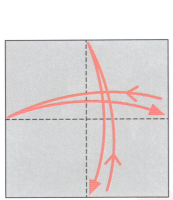

1 Fold the paper in half edge to edge both ways and unfold to make 2 creases.

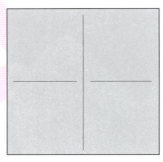

Step ① is completed. Turn the paper over.

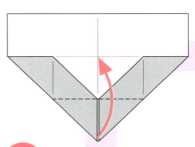

5 Fold the bottom corner up so that the point aligns with the adjacent edges.

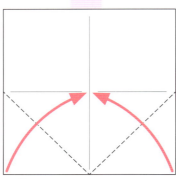

Turn over

2 Fold the bottom corners to the center.

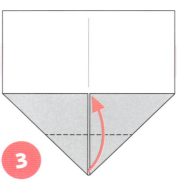

3 Fold the bottom corner to the center.

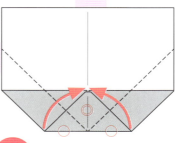

4 Fold the edge marked with ○ symbols to align with the crease marked with ○.

110 Chapter 5

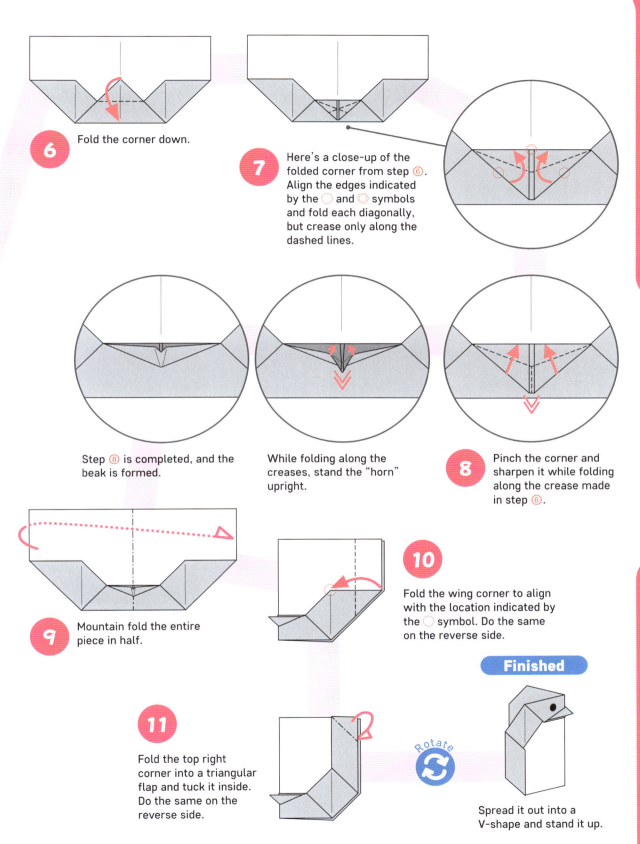

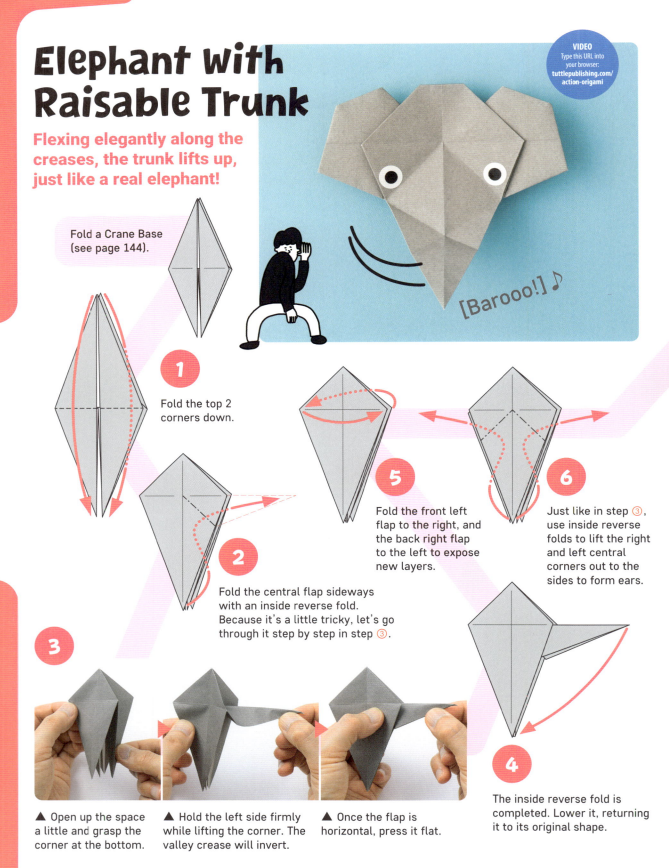

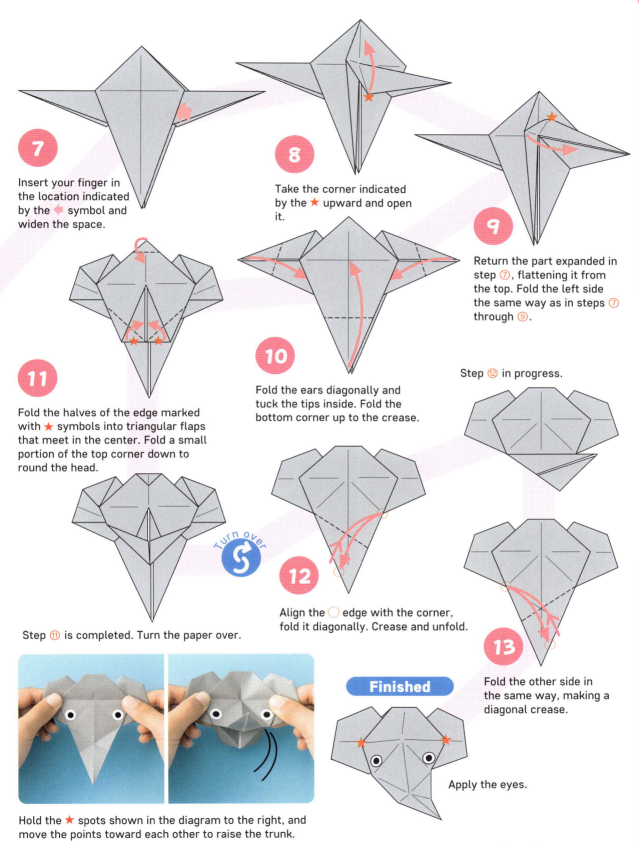

Cute Chibi Animals   113

Bouncing Squid

Did you know? Squid swim in the water by scooting in little arcs using jets of water that they produce!

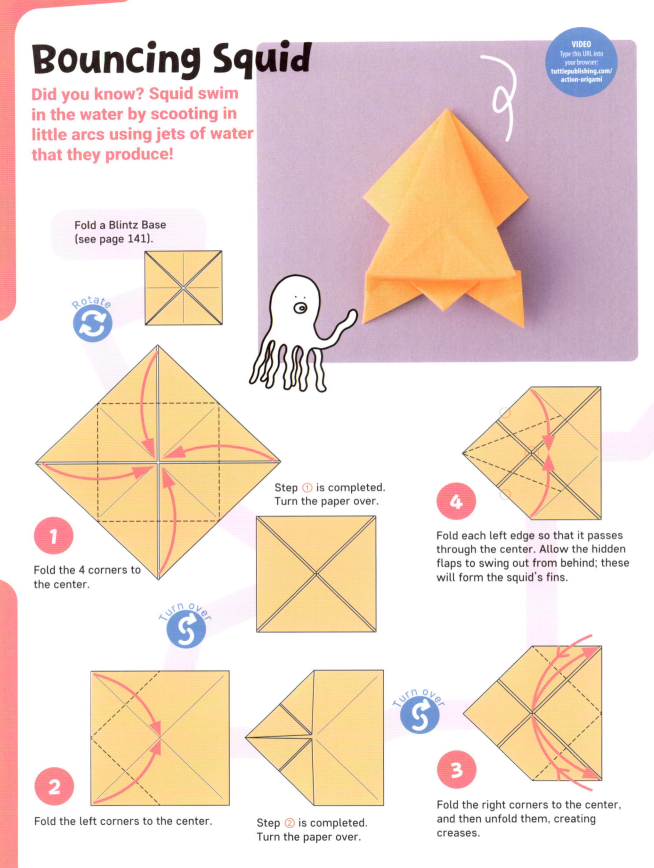

Fold a Blintz Base (see page 141).

1 Fold the 4 corners to the center.

Step ① is completed. Turn the paper over.

2 Fold the left corners to the center.

Step ② is completed. Turn the paper over.

3 Fold the right corners to the center, and then unfold them, creating creases.

4 Fold each left edge so that it passes through the center. Allow the hidden flaps to swing out from behind; these will form the squid's fins.

114 Chapter 5

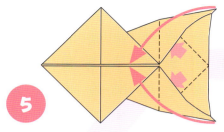

When you open up the interior, the corner will rise, so flatten it to the left.

5 Insert your fingers in the locations indicated by the ← symbols, open up the inside, and bring the right corners to the center and flatten them.

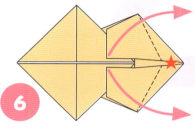

6 Press down firmly so that the ★ corner doesn't open, and then fold back the corners created in step ⑤.

Sharpen the folds to form 2 tentacles.

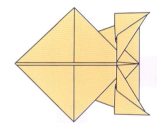

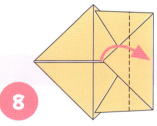

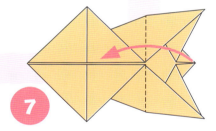

Step ⑧ is completed.

8 Fold the flap to the right. Be careful not to let the middle triangle stick out beyond the edge; if it does, the squid won't hop well.

7 Fold the body to the left along a line that passes by the end of the seam.

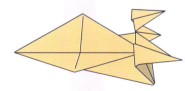

Side view. The tentacles will act as a spring.

Finished

Bounce the Squid by pressing down on the back and sliding your finger off of the back edge.

Cute Chibi Animals 115

Dancing Octopus

This lively octopus lifts its arms to wave them. Make it dance to music!

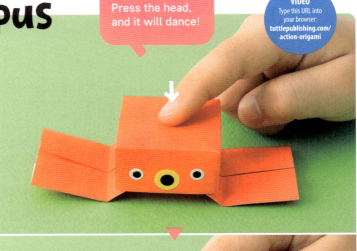

Press the head, and it will dance!

VIDEO Type this URL into your browser: tuttlepublishing.com/action-origami

Fold an 8-Row Precrease (1) (see page 142).

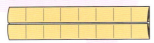

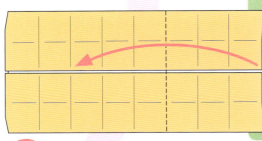

1 Open the paper into this shape, and then fold the 3 columns from the right to the left.

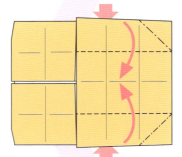

2 Insert your fingers in the locations indicated by the symbols, widen the spaces, and then fold the top and bottom rows to the center, flattening them.

4 Fold the 3 columns from the left to the right.

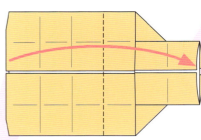

3 Fold the flap formed in step ② back to the right.

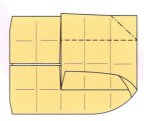

Step ② in progress.

116 Chapter 5

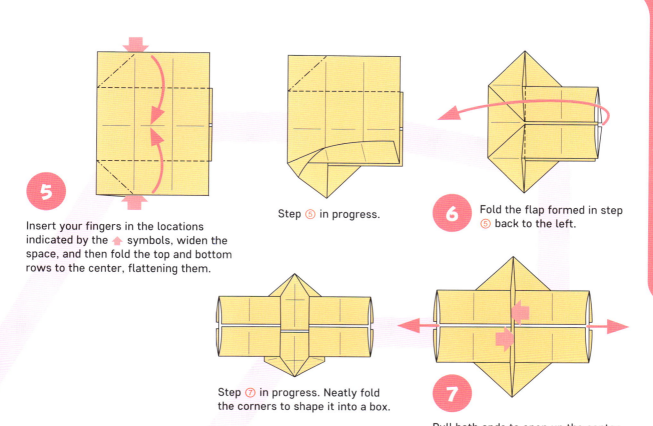

5 Insert your fingers in the locations indicated by the ⬆ symbols, widen the space, and then fold the top and bottom rows to the center, flattening them.

Step ⑤ in progress.

6 Fold the flap formed in step ⑤ back to the left.

Step ⑦ in progress. Neatly fold the corners to shape it into a box.

7 Pull both ends to open up the center.

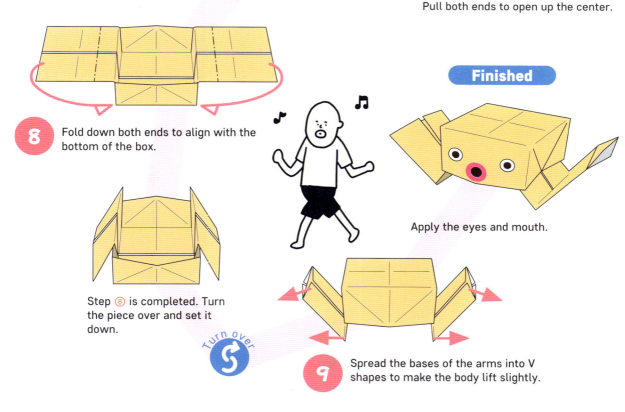

8 Fold down both ends to align with the bottom of the box.

Step ⑧ is completed. Turn the piece over and set it down.

Finished

Apply the eyes and mouth.

9 Spread the bases of the arms into V shapes to make the body lift slightly.

Cute Chibi Animals 117

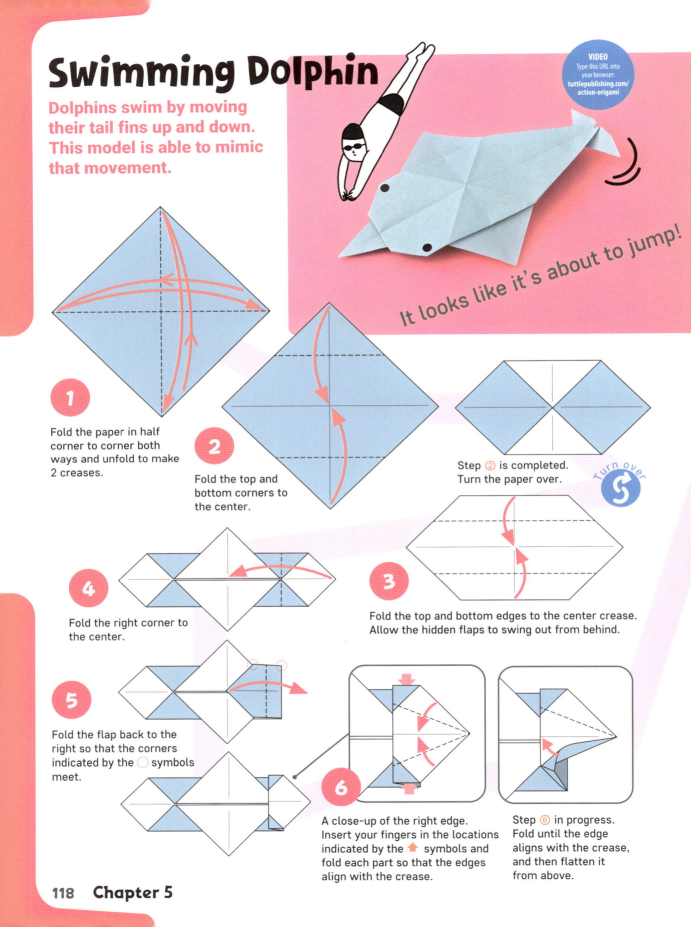

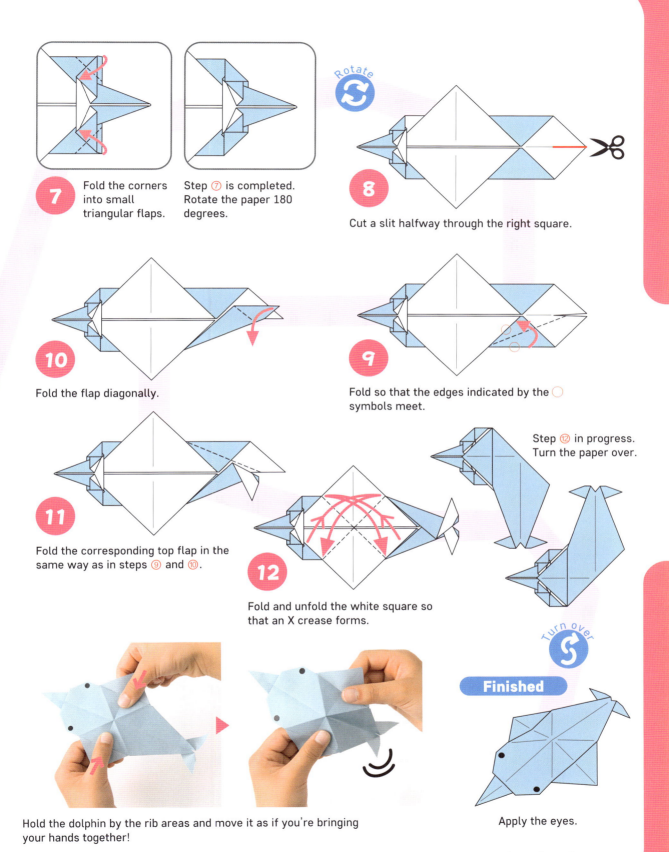

Happy Squirrel

Why is it called "Happy"? You'll understand when you fold it, but suffice it to say that it's just an excitable squirrel.

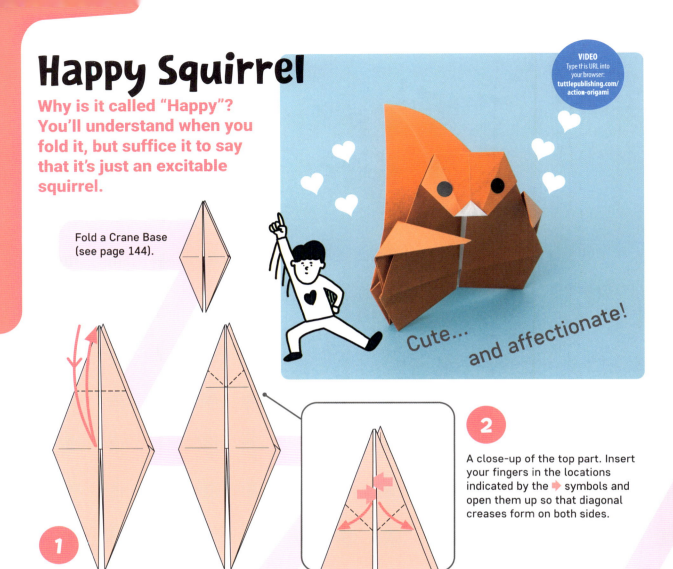

Cute... and affectionate!

Fold a Crane Base (see page 144).

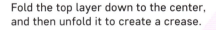

1 Fold the top layer down to the center, and then unfold it to create a crease.

2 A close-up of the top part. Insert your fingers in the locations indicated by the ➡ symbols and open them up so that diagonal creases form on both sides.

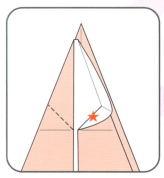

Step ② in progress. Firmly press at the ★ spot to make a strong crease.

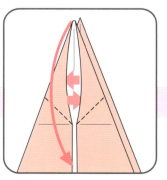

3 Use the creases made in step ② to fold down the top corner and flatten it.

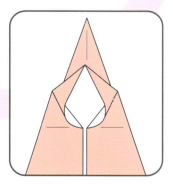

Step ③ in progress. Flatten it downward as shown.

120 **Chapter 5**

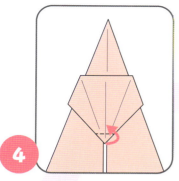
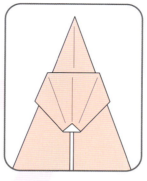

4
The Squirrel's face is now formed. Fold the bottom corner into a small triangular flap to form the nose.

Step ④ is completed.

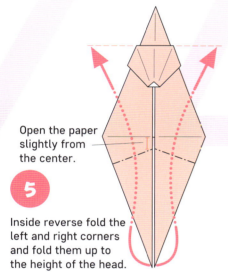
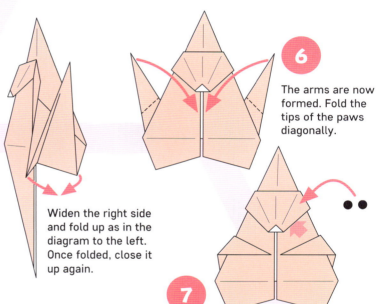

Open the paper slightly from the center.

5
Inside reverse fold the left and right corners and fold them up to the height of the head.

Widen the right side and fold up as in the diagram to the left. Once folded, close it up again.

6
The arms are now formed. Fold the tips of the paws diagonally.

7
Insert your finger in the location indicated by the ⬆ symbol to raise the face. Apply the eyes.

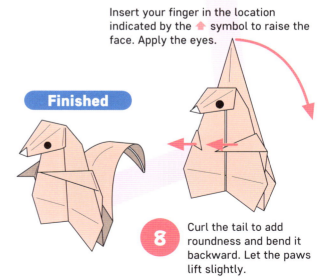

It sways and moves excitedly ☆

Hold the curled tail to wiggle the Squirrel.

Finished

8
Curl the tail to add roundness and bend it backward. Let the paws lift slightly.

Cute Chibi Animals   121

Howling Dog

This origami dog is suddenly possessed by the urge to howl! Help it to call its friends with its baying!

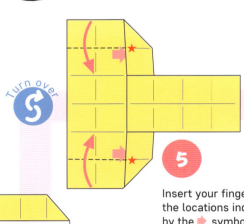

Firmly press your fingers together!

[Woof!]

Fold an 8-Row Precrease (2) (see page 142).

1
Insert your fingers between the folds and diagonally fold the fourth squares from the right to open up the inside.

2
Swing the part that raises up to the right and flatten it.

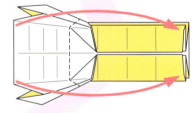

3
Insert your fingers in the locations indicated by the ⬆ symbols and expand the areas indicated by the ★ symbols from the inside.

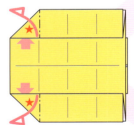

4
Swivel the part that has risen to the left this time, and flatten it again.

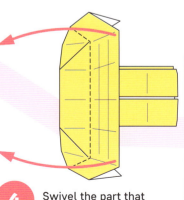

Step ④ is completed. Turn the paper over.

5
Insert your fingers in the locations indicated by the ➡ symbols and expand the areas indicated by the ★ symbols, folding in the top and bottom edges.

122   Chapter 5

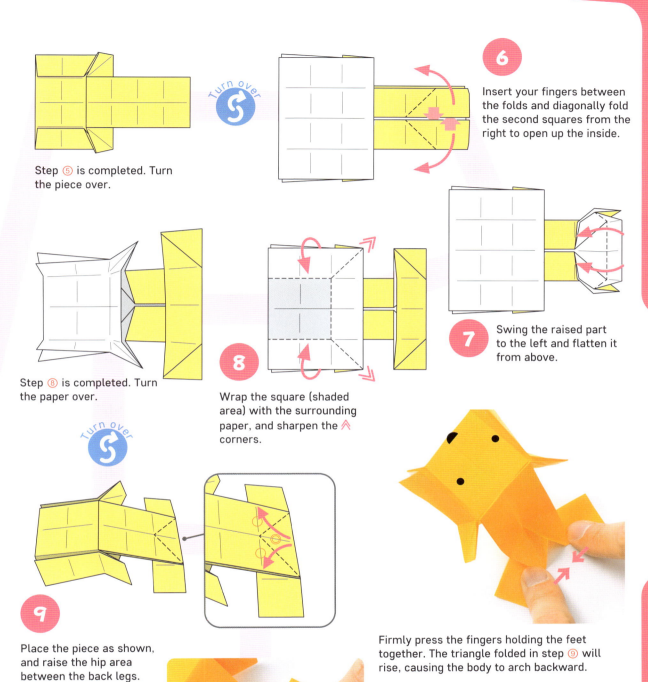

Step ⑤ is completed. Turn the piece over.

6 Insert your fingers between the folds and diagonally fold the second squares from the right to open up the inside.

7 Swing the raised part to the left and flatten it from above.

Step ⑧ is completed. Turn the paper over.

8 Wrap the square (shaded area) with the surrounding paper, and sharpen the ⋀ corners.

9 Place the piece as shown, and raise the hip area between the back legs. Align the ◯ and ◯ creases and fold diagonally at 2 points.

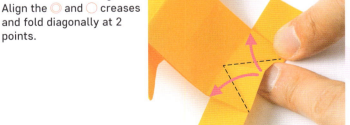

Insert your finger from below and lift diagonally.

Firmly press the fingers holding the feet together. The triangle folded in step ⑨ will rise, causing the body to arch backward.

Finished

Exercise the ear creases to define them, and apply the eyes and nose.

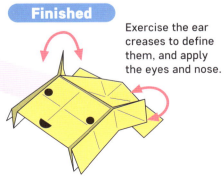

Cute Chibi Animals

Flipping Frog

The more it jumps, the more it flips over—it's just a clumsy frog!

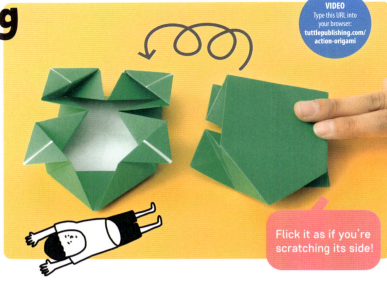

Flick it as if you're scratching its side!

VIDEO
Type this URL into your browser:
tuttlepublishing.com/action-origami

With the white side of the origami paper facing up, fold up to step ② of the Self-Destruct Button (2) (page 80).

1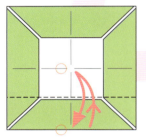
Align the edge with the center crease, fold it, and then unfold.

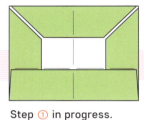
Step ① in progress.

2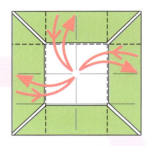
Fold and unfold the edges of the other 3 sides in the same way.

5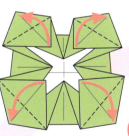
Fold the 4 corners outward into triangular flaps. These will form the leg springs.

4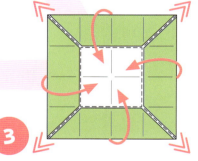
Insert your fingers into the 4 "horns," open them up, and press them toward the center.

3
Fold the surrounding areas around the center square. This will cause the corners to stand up like horns.

6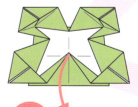
Pull one of the inner corners outward.

Step ⑥ is completed. Turn the piece over.

Finished
 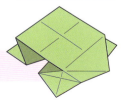

124   Chapter 5

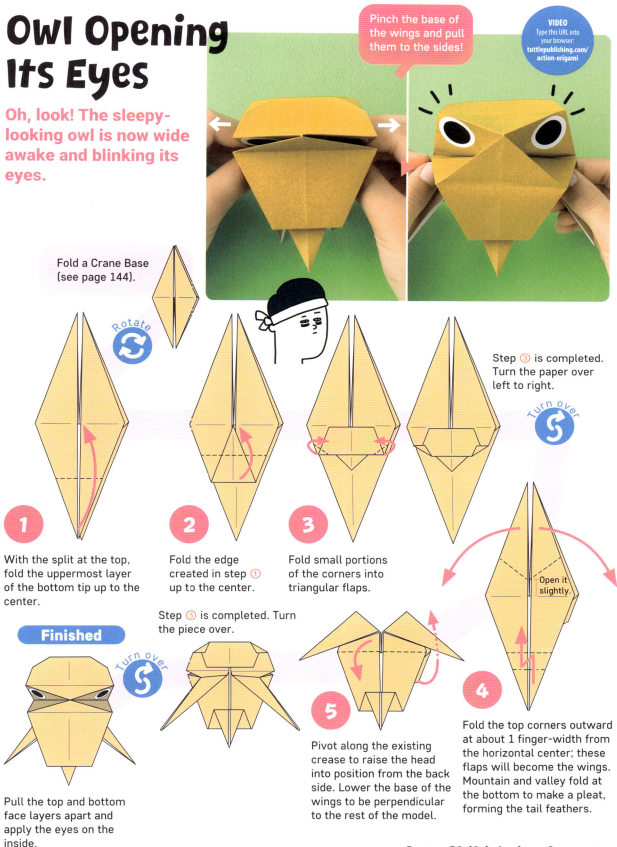

Lovey-Dovey Fox

Two foxes come close... and then kiss! ♡ **Let's help them nuzzle affectionately!**

Adjust the pressure with your fingers carefully!

VIDEO Type this URL into your browser: tuttlepublishing.com/action-origami

Fold an 8-Row Precrease (2) (see page 142).

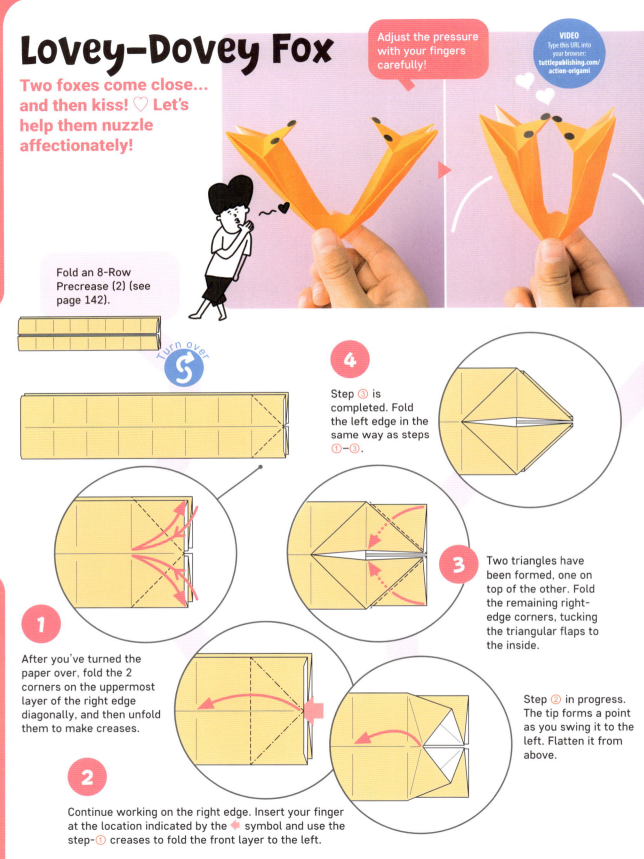

1 After you've turned the paper over, fold the 2 corners on the uppermost layer of the right edge diagonally, and then unfold them to make creases.

2 Continue working on the right edge. Insert your finger at the location indicated by the ⬅ symbol and use the step-① creases to fold the front layer to the left.

3 Two triangles have been formed, one on top of the other. Fold the remaining right-edge corners, tucking the triangular flaps to the inside.

Step ② in progress. The tip forms a point as you swing it to the left. Flatten it from above.

4 Step ③ is completed. Fold the left edge in the same way as steps ①–③.

126   Chapter 5

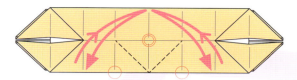

5 Align the ◯ edges with the center ◯ crease, fold each **diagonally**, and then unfold. This will make a V-shaped crease.

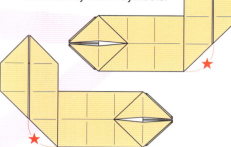

Step ⑤ in progress. Only crease along the spans indicated by the ★ symbols.

6 Just like in step ⑤, create a mirroring V-shaped crease on the top half.

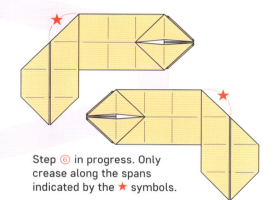

Step ⑥ in progress. Only crease along the spans indicated by the ★ symbols.

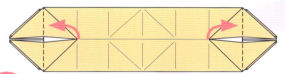

7 A ◇ crease has formed in the center. Lift up the 2 corners on either side, making them perpendicular.

Finished

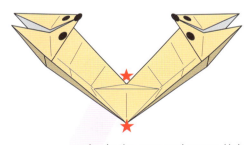

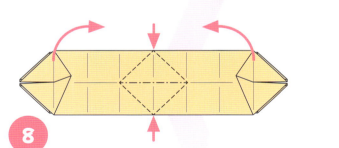

8 Push in from both sides of the ◇ crease to make it three-dimensional and lift the sides into a U shape.

Apply the eyes and noses. Hold the ★ spots and activate the smooching maneuver!

When you gently pinch to press the ◇ spot, the sides automatically lift up.

Cute Chibi Animals   127

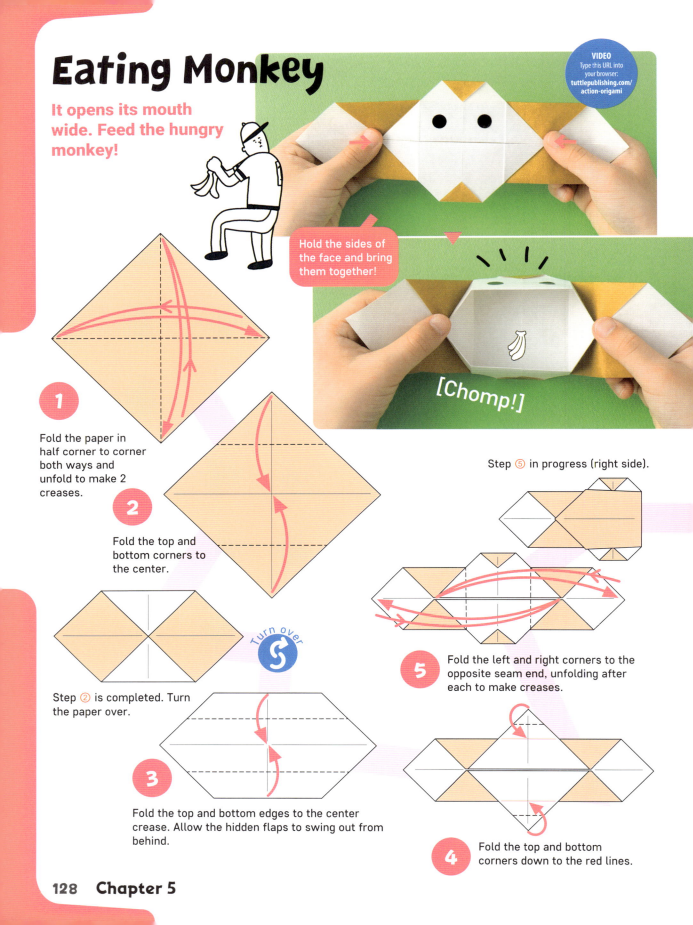

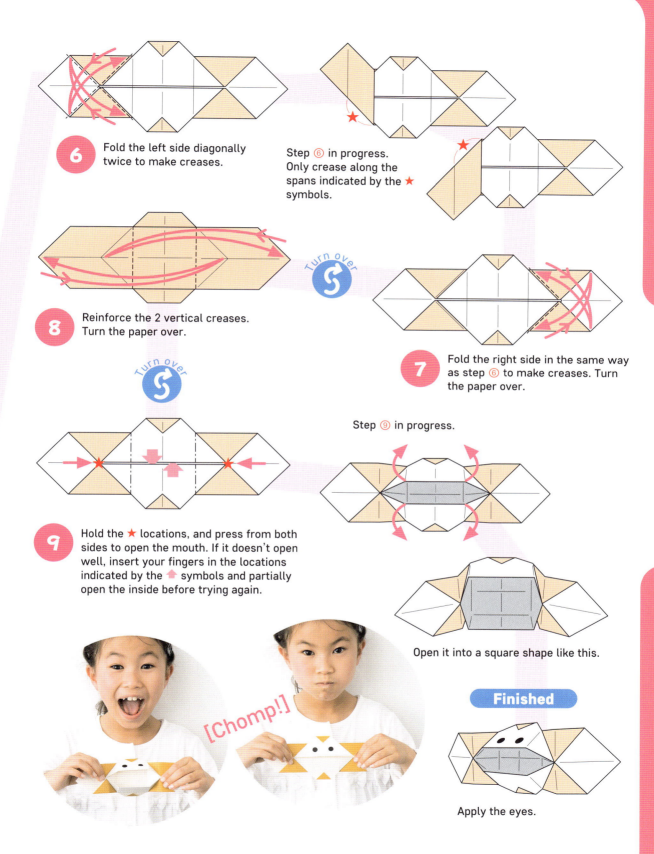

Cute Chibi Animals

Gliding Cat

The cute box-shaped kitty slides smoothly as it scoots.

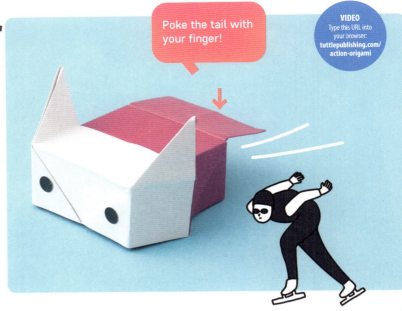

Poke the tail with your finger!

VIDEO Type this URL into your browser: tuttlepublishing.com/action-origami

Fold an 8-Row Precrease (1) (see page 142).

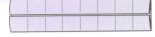

1 Open the paper into this shape, and then fold the 3 columns from the right to the left.

2 Insert your fingers in the locations indicated by the ⬆ symbols, widen the spaces, and then fold the top and bottom rows to the center, flattening them.

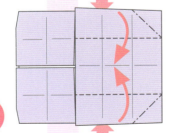

Step ② in progress.

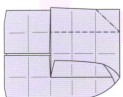

3 Fold the flaps to the outside.

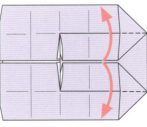

4 Fold 2 columns to the right.

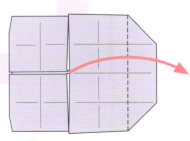

5 Fold the flaps to the center.

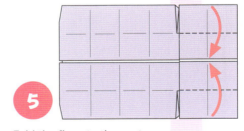

6 Fold the rightmost column to the left.

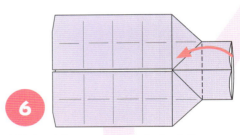

130   Chapter 5

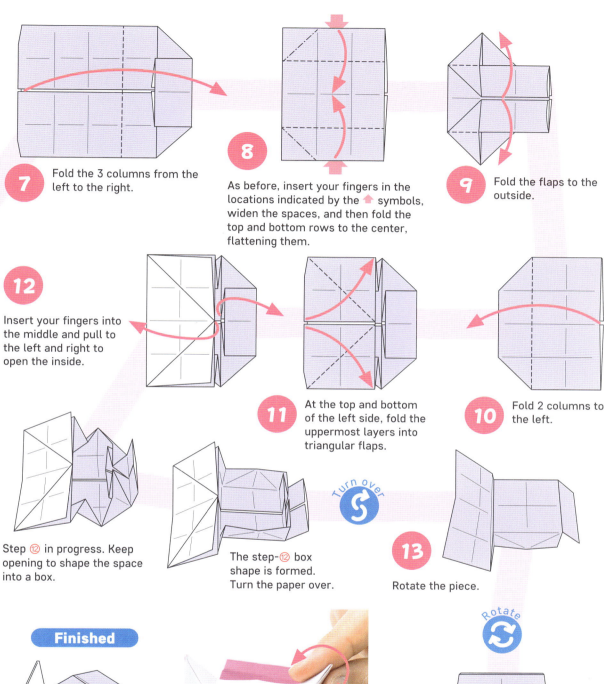

7 Fold the 3 columns from the left to the right.

8 As before, insert your fingers in the locations indicated by the ⬆ symbols, widen the spaces, and then fold the top and bottom rows to the center, flattening them.

9 Fold the flaps to the outside.

12 Insert your fingers into the middle and pull to the left and right to open the inside.

11 At the top and bottom of the left side, fold the uppermost layers into triangular flaps.

10 Fold 2 columns to the left.

Step ⑫ in progress. Keep opening to shape the space into a box.

The step-⑫ box shape is formed. Turn the paper over.

13 Rotate the piece.

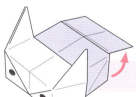

Finished

Lift the tail and apply the eyes.

Pinch the ⋀ corners in the diagram to the right to form the ears. Fold them firmly on both sides.

14 Use the white paper to wrap the box and create the face and ears.

Cute Chibi Animals   131

Pecking Woodpecker

The head bobs vigorously back and forth. Can you move it as fast as the real thing?

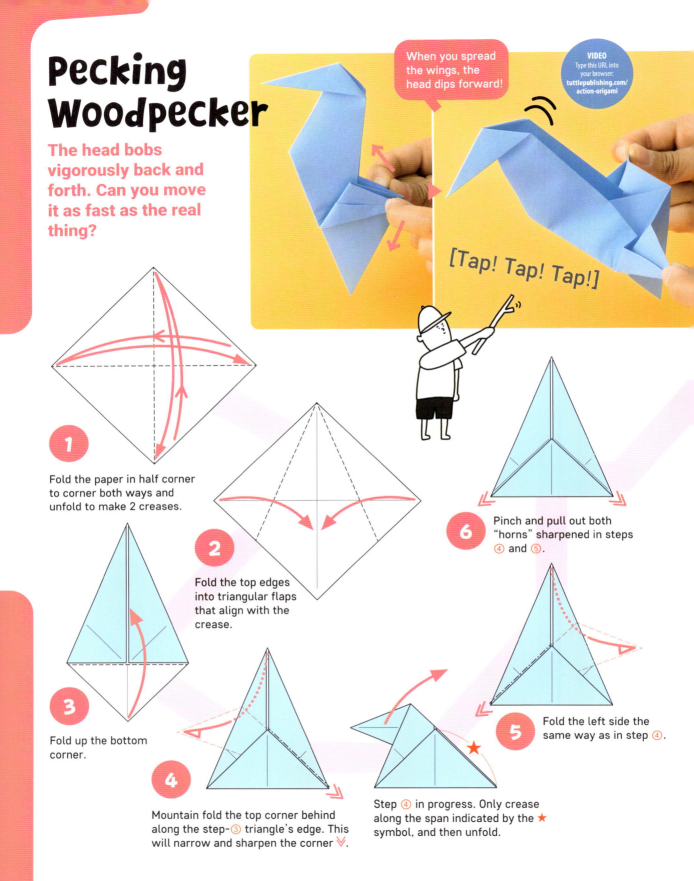

When you spread the wings, the head dips forward!

VIDEO Type this URL into your browser: tuttlepublishing.com/action-origami

[Tap! Tap! Tap!]

1 Fold the paper in half corner to corner both ways and unfold to make 2 creases.

2 Fold the top edges into triangular flaps that align with the crease.

3 Fold up the bottom corner.

4 Mountain fold the top corner behind along the step-③ triangle's edge. This will narrow and sharpen the corner ⋁.

Step ④ in progress. Only crease along the span indicated by the ★ symbol, and then unfold.

5 Fold the left side the same way as in step ④.

6 Pinch and pull out both "horns" sharpened in steps ④ and ⑤.

132   Chapter 5

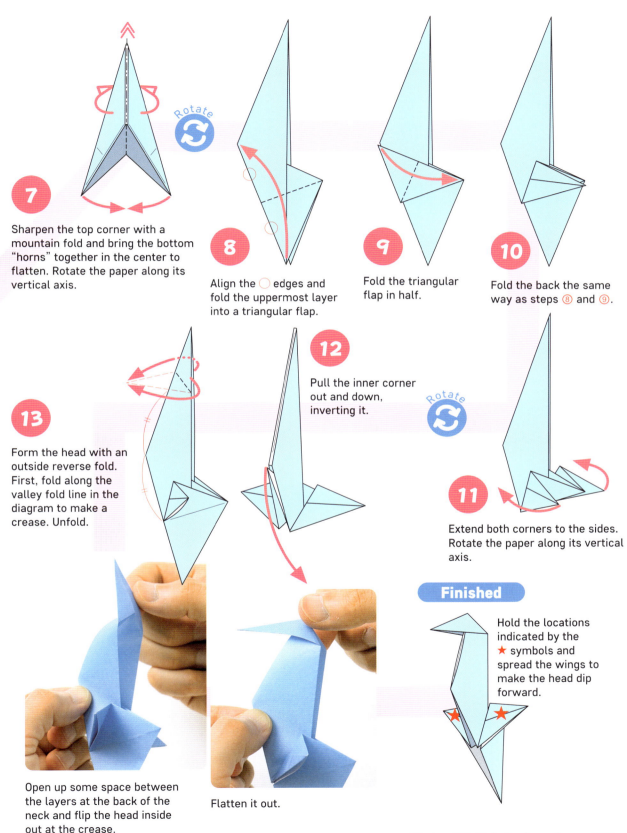

7 Sharpen the top corner with a mountain fold and bring the bottom "horns" together in the center to flatten. Rotate the paper along its vertical axis.

8 Align the ○ edges and fold the uppermost layer into a triangular flap.

9 Fold the triangular flap in half.

10 Fold the back the same way as steps ⑧ and ⑨.

12 Pull the inner corner out and down, inverting it.

13 Form the head with an outside reverse fold. First, fold along the valley fold line in the diagram to make a crease. Unfold.

11 Extend both corners to the sides. Rotate the paper along its vertical axis.

Finished Hold the locations indicated by the ★ symbols and spread the wings to make the head dip forward.

Open up some space between the layers at the back of the neck and flip the head inside out at the crease.

Flatten it out.

Cute Chibi Animals 133

Gliding Ray

Simulate the appearance of a graceful ray leisurely swimming in the sea, flapping its large fins.

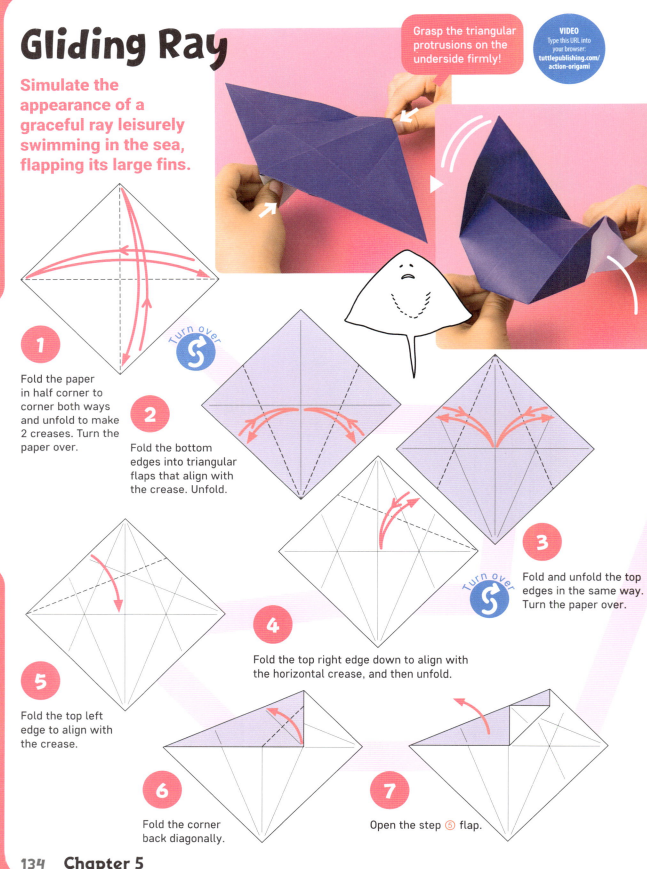

Grasp the triangular protrusions on the underside firmly!

VIDEO Type this URL into your browser: tuttlepublishing.com/action-origami

1 Fold the paper in half corner to corner both ways and unfold to make 2 creases. Turn the paper over.

2 Fold the bottom edges into triangular flaps that align with the crease. Unfold.

3 Fold and unfold the top edges in the same way. Turn the paper over.

4 Fold the top right edge down to align with the horizontal crease, and then unfold.

5 Fold the top left edge to align with the crease.

6 Fold the corner back diagonally.

7 Open the step ⑤ flap.

134   Chapter 5

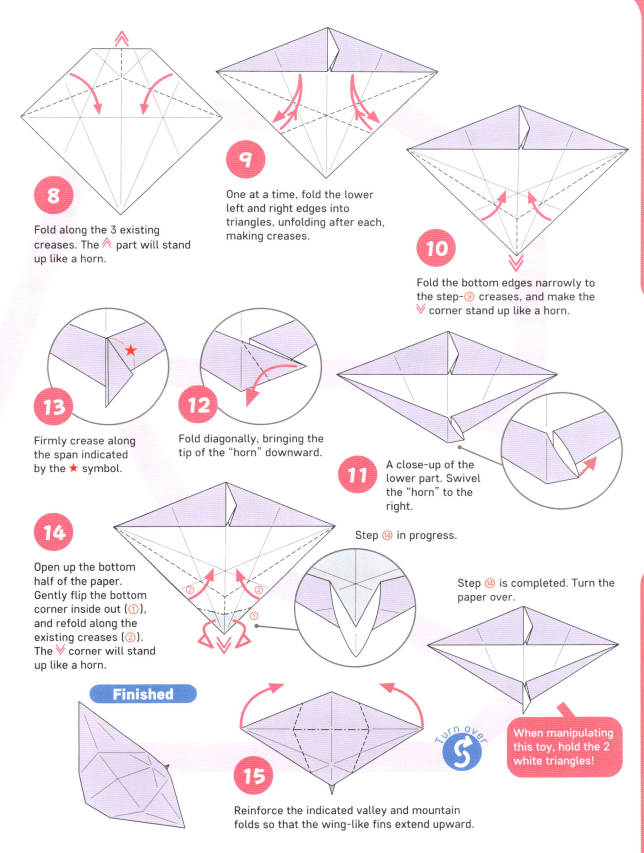

Cute Chibi Animals   135

Somersault Seal

This acrobatic *pinniped* ("flipper-foot) will show off with an impressive somersault!

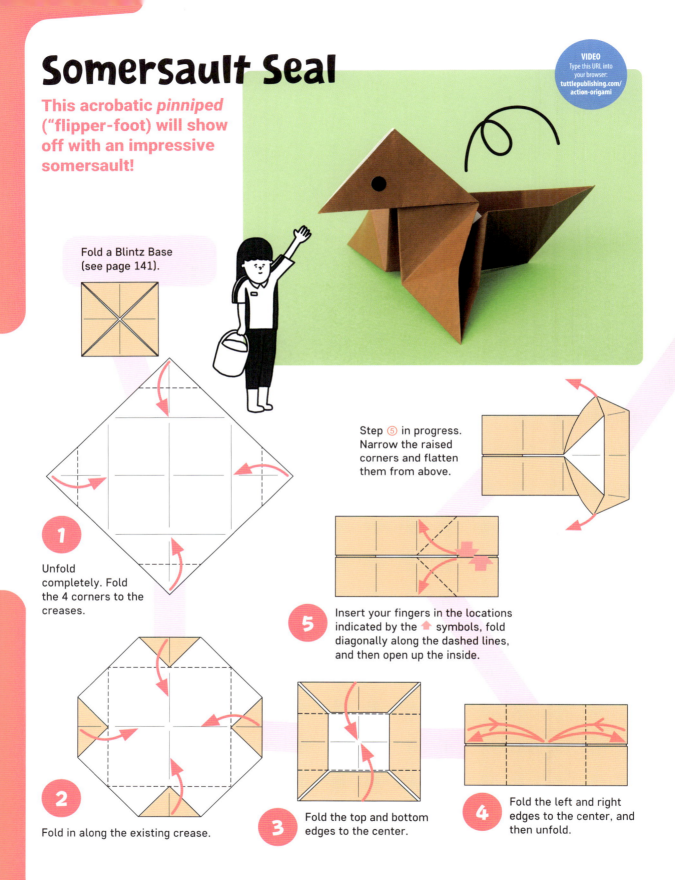

Fold a Blintz Base (see page 141).

1 Unfold completely. Fold the 4 corners to the creases.

2 Fold in along the existing crease.

3 Fold the top and bottom edges to the center.

4 Fold the left and right edges to the center, and then unfold.

5 Insert your fingers in the locations indicated by the ⬆ symbols, fold diagonally along the dashed lines, and then open up the inside.

Step ⑤ in progress. Narrow the raised corners and flatten them from above.

VIDEO
Type this URL into your browser:
tuttlepublishing.com/action-origami

136 Chapter 5

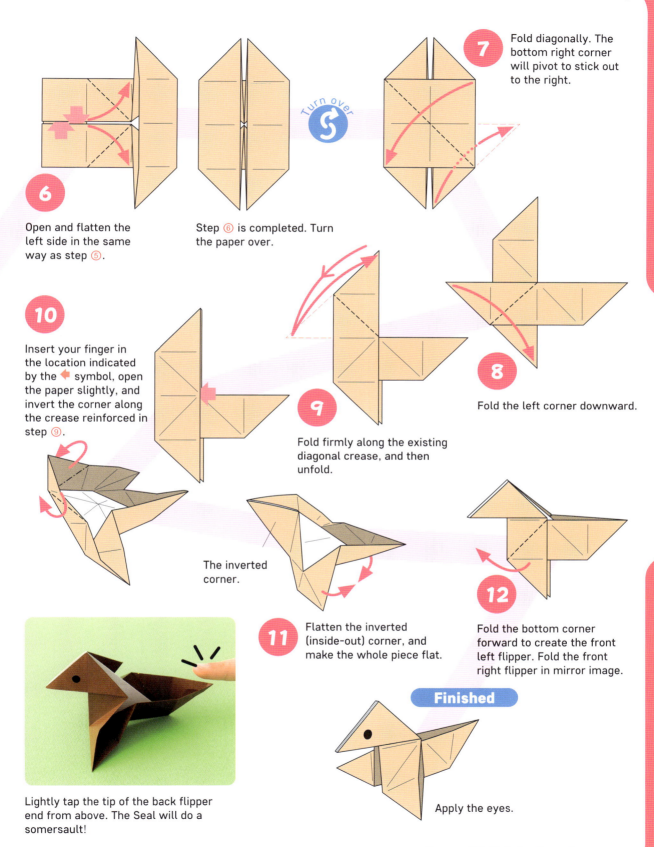

Cute Chibi Animals 137

Munching Fish

Watch out! This big fish will chomp down with its gaping mouth.

Will you be swallowed whole with one big gulp!?

VIDEO Type this URL into your browser: tuttlepublishing.com/action-origami

Fold a Blintz Base (see page 141).

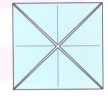

Turn over

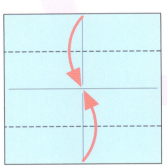

1 Fold the top and bottom edges to the center.

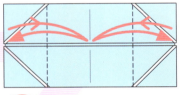

2 Fold the left and right edges to the center, and then unfold to make creases.

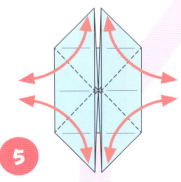

5 Swing the 4 corners in the opposite directions, making strong creases.

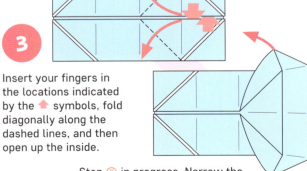

3 Insert your fingers in the locations indicated by the ↑ symbols, fold diagonally along the dashed lines, and then open up the inside.

Step ③ in progress. Narrow the raised corners and flatten them from above.

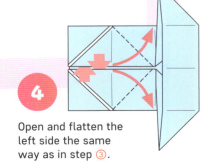

4 Open and flatten the left side the same way as in step ③.

138 Chapter 5

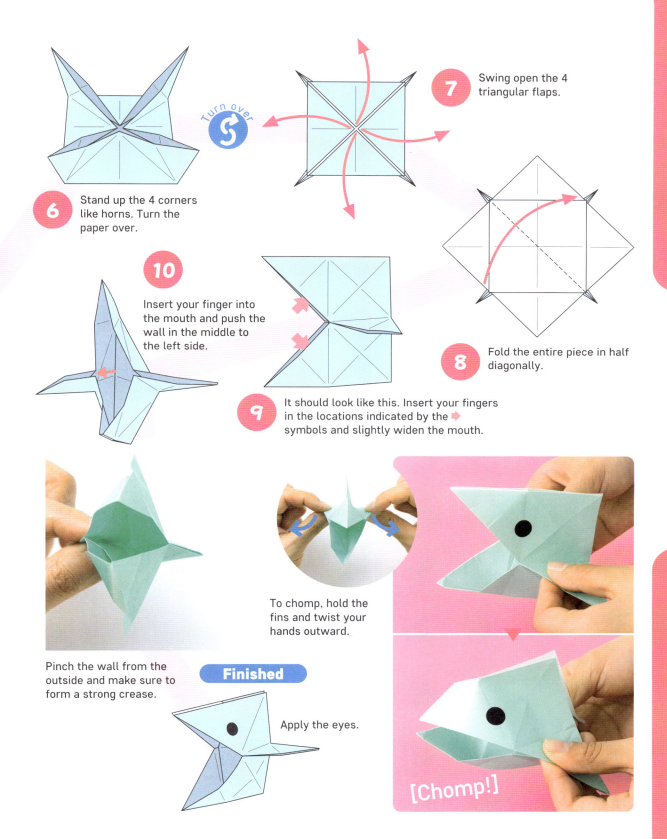

Cute Chibi Animals 139

Swimming Sunfish

The dorsal and pelvic fins will flap just like a real fish.

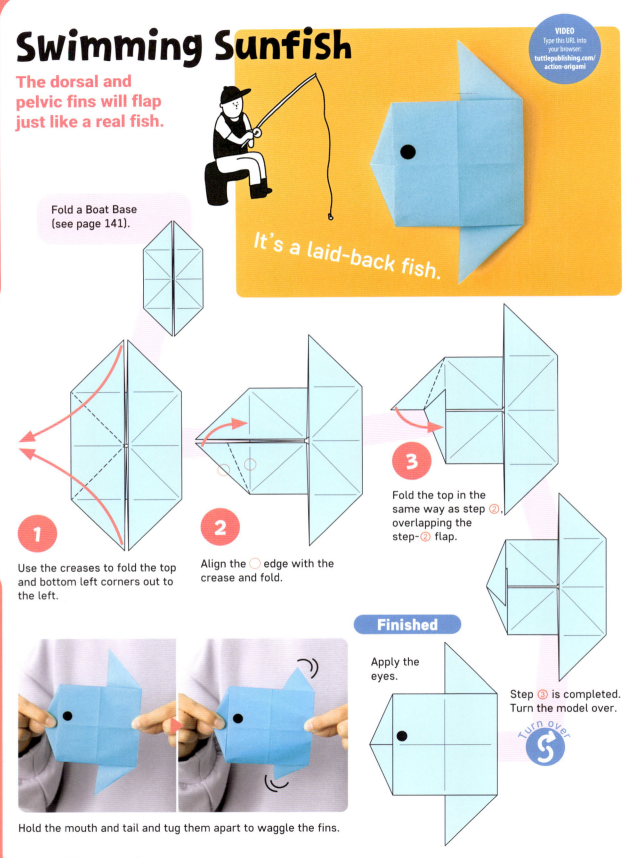

It's a laid-back fish.

Fold a Boat Base (see page 141).

1 Use the creases to fold the top and bottom left corners out to the left.

2 Align the ○ edge with the crease and fold.

3 Fold the top in the same way as step ②, overlapping the step-② flap.

Finished

Apply the eyes.

Step ③ is completed. Turn the model over.

Hold the mouth and tail and tug them apart to **waggle the fins**.

140   Chapter 5

Origami Bases

Here's how to fold the origami bases that are used at the beginning of many projects.

Blintz Base

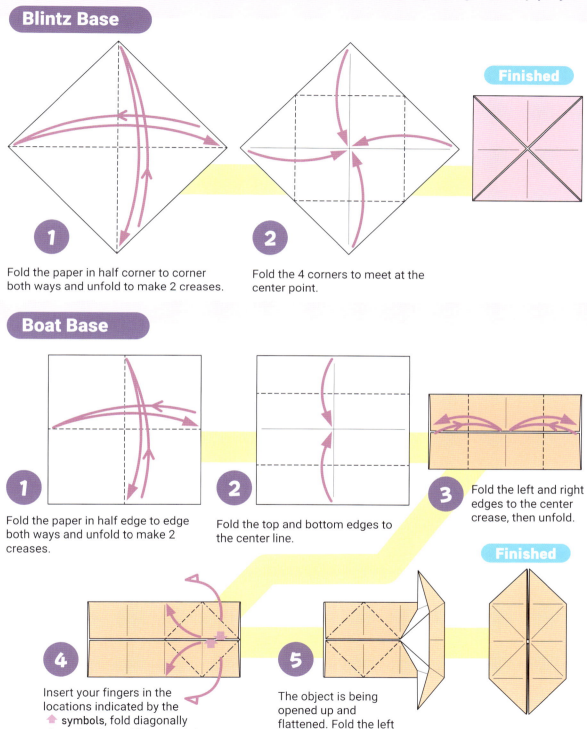

1 Fold the paper in half corner to corner both ways and unfold to make 2 creases.

2 Fold the 4 corners to meet at the center point.

Boat Base

1 Fold the paper in half edge to edge both ways and unfold to make 2 creases.

2 Fold the top and bottom edges to the center line.

3 Fold the left and right edges to the center crease, then unfold.

4 Insert your fingers in the locations indicated by the ⬆ **symbols**, fold diagonally along the dashed lines, and then open up the inside and flatten.

5 The object is being opened up and flattened. Fold the left half in the same way.

141

8-Row Precrease (1)

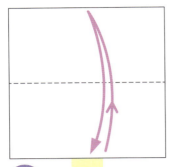

1 Fold the paper in half and unfold to make a crease.

4 Unfold completely. Rotate the paper.

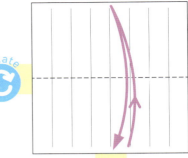

5 With the paper oriented with the creases running vertically, repeat steps ①–③.

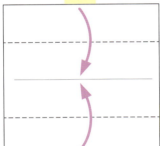

2 Fold the top and bottom edges to the center crease.

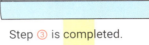

Step ③ is completed.

3 Fold the top and bottom edges to the center crease again.

Finished

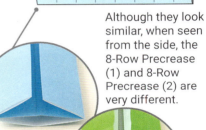

Although they look similar, when seen from the side, the 8-Row Precrease (1) and 8-Row Precrease (2) are very different.

8-Row Precrease (1)

8-Row Precrease (2)

8-Row Precrease (2)

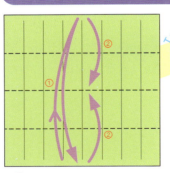

1 Follow the directions for 8-Row Precrease (1) up to step ④, and turn the paper over so that the colored side is facing up and the creases are vertical. Fold in half and unfold to make a crease (①), and fold the top and bottom edges to the center crease (②). Turn the paper over.

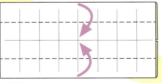

2 Fold in the top and bottom edges to the center crease. However, do not fold the paper in the back—leave it unfolded.

Only the upper layer is folded. Creases are not made on the back layer of paper.

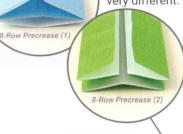

Finished

3 Fold the top and bottom edges to the center crease.

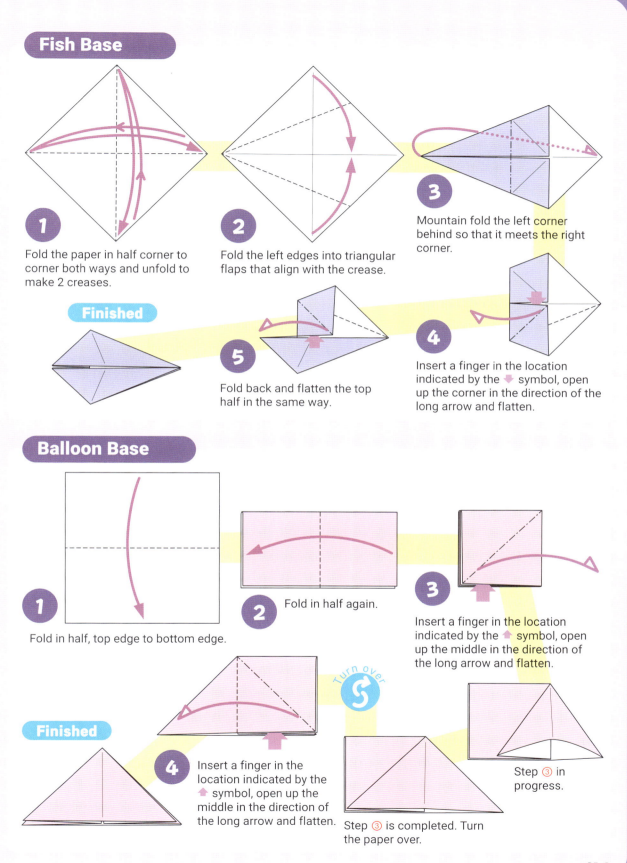

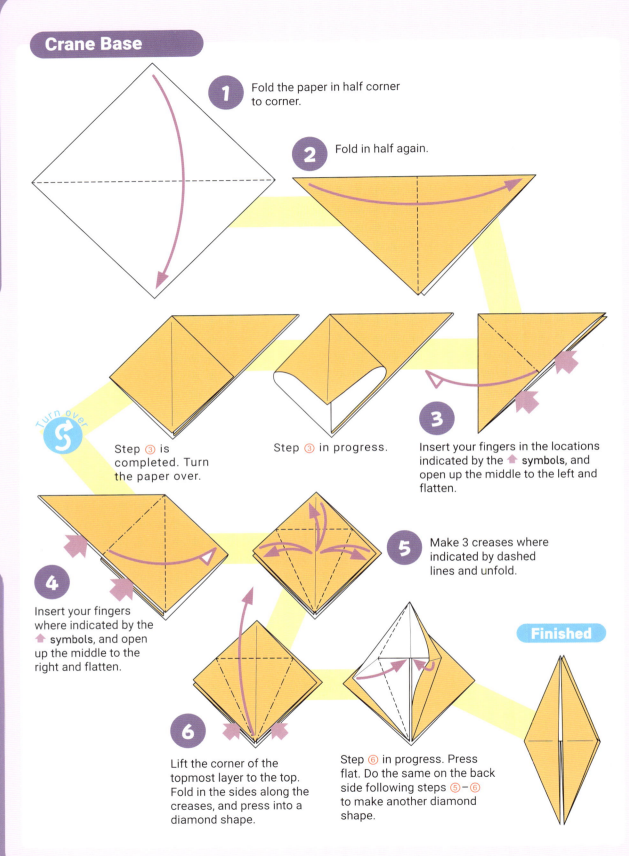